The MIRACLE MORNING *for* COUPLES

Create Legendary Connection One Morning at a Time

Hal Elrod • Lance & Brandy Salazar

With Honorée Corder

Hal Elrod & Lance and Brandy Salazar with Honorée Corder

Paperback ISBN: 978-1-942589-29-7

E book IBSN: 978-1-942589-31-0

Interior Design: Dino Marino, www.dinomarino.com

DEDICATIONS

Hal

This book is dedicated to my wife for life, Ursula Elrod. You are truly my best friend *and* the woman of my dreams! I love and appreciate you more every single day, and I am so grateful that we get to co-create and share this life together!

Lance and Brandy

This book is dedicated to our daughters, Hooley and Natalie. Thank you for being a reason to fight for our marriage in a way that shows you what is possible. And for your patience while we attempted to homeschool you both as we wrote this book.

We love you!

CONTENTS

A first look at the Four Legendary Relationship Elements and The Partnership Loop. Learn what makes our intimate relationships so challenging and why the Miracle Morning can be used to make them legendary.

Section I: You and The Miracle Morning

The art and science of why mornings are the key to changing your life and your relationship for the better.

How to actually wake up when the alarm goes off, going from being a snooze-a-holic to early bird in five minutes.

The last Element is the pinnacle of intimacy. Learn how to foster deep vulnerability and trust by becoming the best of lovers.

Section IV: Becoming a Legendary Couple

Put all the pieces together so the two of you can make a plan and take action to create the relationship you desire.

Kick off your journey together with a 3-phase strategy to implement any habit in one month.

A SPECIAL INVITATION FROM HAL

Readers and practitioners of *The Miracle Morning* have co-created an extraordinary community consisting of over 180,000+ like-minded individuals, from around the world, who wake up each day *with purpose* and dedicate time to fulfilling the unlimited potential that is within all of us while helping others to do the same.

As the author of *The Miracle Morning*, I felt that I had a responsibility to create an online community where readers could come together to connect, get encouragement, share best practices, support one another, discuss the book, post videos, find an accountability partner, and even swap smoothie recipes and exercise routines.

However, I honestly had no idea that The Miracle Morning Community would become one of the most positive, engaged, and supportive online communities in the world, but it has. I'm constantly astounded by the caliber and the character of our members, which presently includes people from over seventy countries and is growing daily.

To join the Miracle Morning Community, just go to **MyT-MMCommunity.com** and request to join The Miracle Morning Community on Facebook. You'll immediately be able to connect with 150,000+ people who are already practicing The Miracle Morning (TMM). While you'll find many who are just beginning their Miracle Morning journey, you'll find even more who have been at it for years, and who will happily share advice, support, and guidance to accelerate your success.

I'll be moderating the community and checking in regularly, so I look forward to seeing you there! If you'd like to connect with me personally on social media, just follow **@HalElrod** on Twitter and **Facebook.com/YoPalHal** on Facebook. Let's connect soon!

FOREWORD
By Hal and Ursula Elrod

Ursula and I have been together for 15 years and happily married for the last ten. But the way our relationship began doesn't exactly lend itself to the stuff of fairy tales.

Well, to be fair, that's mostly because Hal had to grow and mature around the idea of a commitment to one woman for the rest of his life. It is a big decision that shouldn't be taken lightly. So, while at the time it was painful for me to go through, looking back, I'm grateful we did because it laid the foundation for the security of our relationship now.

That's definitely fair. I take responsibility for our rocky start. I was navigating my way through my own "commitment" issues. I believed you were "the one," but I needed more time than you did to come to that conclusion. Yes, we had to overcome a lot of challenges together, but it was all worth it and wouldn't you say that our relationship has turned out to be everything we hoped it would be?

Absolutely. Our relationship really has become everything I dreamt it could be. I just want to make sure that the person reading this understands that no relationship is ever perfect, and it took us a looonnggg time and a lot of work to get to the point of harmony. It's still not perfect. We still disagree, but at the end of the day our love is deep and our commitment unwavering.

Very true. And that's why I'm excited for them to read this book. In fact, if you're reading this, that means that you are just a few pages away from meeting two of the most evolved human beings who form one of the most evolved couples that Ursula and I have ever had the pleasure of knowing, my co-authors who have also become close friends, Lance and Brandy Salazar.

You'll first have the opportunity to read their *Notes*, in which you'll immediately experience their authenticity and vulnerability. Like Ursula and I, they had to go *through* it before they could get *to* it. The *it* they had to go through was facing nearly marriage-ending differences and conflicts. Then each realizing that they needed to acknowledge and take responsibility for their own individual shortcomings and grow beyond those shortcomings (something all of us can learn from and model). The *it* they got to represents where they are now—in a relationship/marriage that is as harmonious and loving and connected as any couple would ever dream of being.

Are they perfect? They'll be the first to tell you that the answer to that is a reasonably strong "no" and that being perfect isn't their objective, nor the point. The point is that together, through years of hard work and an unwavering commitment to making their marriage thrive, Lance and Brandy have created a powerful approach to their life as a couple. It has truly made their relationship legendary and helped Ursula and I do the same for ours. Now, their approach—contained in this book—has the power to do the same for you and *your* relationship, no matter what stage it's at in the present moment.

For each book in the Miracle Morning series, I strive to partner with co-authors who exemplify both the values and wisdom that I believe will be transformative for you. In the case of *The Miracle Morning for Couples*, whether you are married, single, divorced, engaged, or somewhere in between, this book is designed to give you the step-by-step framework to both transform yourself *and* your relationship(s). But first, if you're okay with it, I'd like to share the two most significant breakthroughs I've had related to my relationship with Ursula, that have made the most profound impact for us.

How does that sound, sweetheart?

I'm curious as to which of your "breakthroughs" you're going to share. It seems like you have a new one almost every day, so this should be good!

Ha-ha. Touché. Well, each of these has been a game-changer for us. So, here goes…

Hal's 1ˢᵗ Relationship Breakthrough: *Selflessly Add Value for Your Significant Other*

Way back in 2004, I defined my purpose in life: *to selflessly add value to the lives of every person that I encounter.* Reinforced daily through affirmations, this purpose became my North Star that has guided all my choices and behavior and has continued to do so for 15 years. Well, *most* of my choices and behavior.

A few years ago, I had a realization that at first disturbed me, but ultimately transformed how I show up in my relationship with Ursula. The disturbing realization was that I was living my purpose in my work, but *not* in my relationship. I was selflessly adding value (professionally) for my clients, customers, and for hundreds of thousands of members of *The Miracle Morning Community*, but *not* for the person who arguably needed and deserved it from me the most—my wife.

It occurred to me that I—and I think many, if not most couples can relate to this—was in a reciprocity-based relationship, experiencing and creating my relationship through the lens of *reciprocity* (though most often doing so unconsciously). Think about that for a second. Do you tend to reciprocate your partner's mood and behavior? For example, if your significant other is in a bad mood and acting negatively towards you, do you tend to mirror that negativity right back to them?

Or, if on the other hand, your partner is sweet, affectionate and loving toward you, don't you naturally feel inclined to be sweet, affectionate and loving right back to them?

The problem with a reciprocity-based relationship is that one or both partners will often react or speak out of a heightened negative emotion, physical fatigue or a temporary bad mood, rather than from our deepest values and highest truth. What often begins as a relatively insignificant amount of negative interaction (a little nagging, bickering, arguing, feeling annoyed with or neglected by the other person, etc.) can spiral into an all-encompassing relationship based on negative reciprocation, where our default mode is to feel negatively toward our partner.

Realizing this, I made both a decision and an actionable commitment that I would immediately begin living my purpose for Ursula every day, by selflessly adding value to her life, regardless of her mood. To articulate and reinforce my newfound commitment, I wrote the following in the form of an affirmation:

> *My #1 objective in my marriage is to selflessly add value to Ursula's life, every single day, regardless of her mood or behavior. Whether it's something small, like doing the dishes or putting the kids to bed or being romantic by surprising her with flowers or it's something more significant like supporting her goals and dreams; I will actively do things every day that help to make Ursula's life*

easier, most enjoyable, and more fulfilling. And, on the occasion that she's having a tough day or in a bad mood, I will never take it personally nor mirror any negativity, but instead, take it as a cue that I need to work even harder to selflessly add value to her life.

I added the preceding text to my daily affirmations and began reading it every day, during my Miracle Morning practice. In the simplest form, an affirmation is simply a "reminder" of what matters most to us, designed to guide our focus, feelings, and behaviors in the direction of where we want to go. And if I didn't read that affirmation every morning, guess what I'd probably forget to do, more often than not? I'd probably forget to *selflessly add value to Ursula's life* and instead fall back into the trap of a reciprocity-based relationship. But because I read that affirmation (aka "reminder") every day, it prompts me to *do something* that adds value to her life. Most days, it's something simple, like taking on a chore that she would normally do or picking up flowers for her at the grocery store or sending her a sweet video-text when I'm traveling. Occasionally it's a little more elaborate, such as setting up a babysitter to watch our kids and surprising Ursula with an overnight stay-cation at a nice hotel in downtown Austin.

When I stopped basing my behavior on hers and instead made a commitment to selflessly add value to Ursula's life, our relationship began changing for the better. Not instantly, of course. Any time we change our behavior, whether that's in the context of our relationships or an individual behavior such as changing our diet or starting a morning ritual, we must be patient and consistent with our new behavior, over an extended period of time. Only then will we see the results that our change in behavior will generate. When I committed to shift my approach to my marriage to that of selflessly adding value for my wife, no matter what (regardless of her mood or how she treats me), she gradually began to take notice. First, I told her about my newfound approach to our marriage, because I wanted her to be aware of my commitment to be a better husband. And although I didn't ask nor expect her to do anything differently (remember, this isn't about keeping score anymore), she began to see and feel and experience the new and improved husband I had become. In turn, she naturally responded positively. And the timing happened to be crucial.

Two months after I established my commitment to selflessly add value to Ursula's life, every day, regardless of her mood or behavior (remember that last part; it's important), I was diagnosed with a very rare and equally aggressive form of cancer, known as Acute Lymphoblastic Leukemia (ALL). Given a grim 20-30% chance of surviving, Ursula and I embarked on the most difficult year of our life as a couple. We took on what you might call a "patient/caretaker relationship" as I underwent chemotherapy, lost 25% of my body weight, and was sick, living in and out of hospitals, for the better part of a year. Despite being overwhelmed with the fear of losing me and the burden of being thrust into the responsibilities of a single-parent, Ursula dug deep amid our adversity, and she became Super-mom and Super-wife, taking care of me, the kids, and our home. Left with little strength, I struggled to get through each day, and it was Ursula who stepped up to selflessly added value to my life, every day.

I once read that *having a great relationship isn't about finding the perfect partner; it is about being the perfect partner.* I love that! That's what it means to selflessly add value for your significant other. It's not about waiting for them to meet your needs, and only meeting theirs if you feel they're meeting yours. Selflessly adding value for your significant others is about YOU going first and going over and above to make your significant other's life easier, more enjoyable, and more fulfilling.

Hal's 2nd Relationship Breakthrough: *Decide What It Means to Be "Best Friends"*

The first song that Ursula and I danced to at our wedding is the song "Lucky" by Jason Mraz and Colbie Caillat. The chorus contains the words, *Lucky I'm in love with my best friend.* However, I have a confession: although we danced to that song over ten years ago, it wasn't until just a few months ago (better late than never) that I both realized and *decided* that Ursula is literally my best friend. Please allow me to explain.

When you and I each met our significant other for the first time, we had no history with them. However, we quickly become infatuated with our newfound love. The feelings of infatuation are so powerful that they usually overtake any feelings we have about anyone else. At least, for a while. But still, we begin our relationship with no shared experiences... no history... no friendship.

For most of us, we have history with our family, our friends, and even our colleagues—but none with this new person. Over time, we share experiences. Ursula and I have been together for over 15 years and married for 10. One night at dinner, staring at her from across the table, listening to her tell me about her day, watching her laugh, something occurred to me that might occur to you: *I've shared more life experiences with Ursula than any other person.* We've overcome more, together. We've celebrated more, together. We braved the 2008 economic crash together (when we were engaged and pregnant). She stayed with me as my business failed, the bank seized my house, my body fat percentage tripled, and I plummeted into a deep depression. We shared the once-in-a-lifetime experience of having our first child together, our daughter. We shared the once-in-a-lifetime experience of having our second child together, our son. Ursula supported me waking up every day at 3:30 a.m. (for over three years) to write *The Miracle Morning.* She was by my side while I battled cancer in 2017. I realized that we've been there for each other more than anyone else has been there for either of us. Then I *decided* that the woman I'm married to isn't just my wife, or my lover, or just the mother of my children, but that she is unequivocally my best friend in the entire world, and will be for the rest of my life.

As soon as I began to see Ursula as my best friend, *everything* got better! I listen to her differently when she talks, studying and appreciating who she is. We have more fun together, resolve disagreements quickly and smoothly, and I've found that even sex is way better—when you have it with your best friend.

Sweetheart, did I miss anything?

No, no, I think you covered it all (and then some!) Everything you shared is true, I can vouch for all of it. It is amazing how after 15 years together, there are still so many things to learn and discover about each other. Life is always changing and forcing us to change and adapt with it. That's why marriage vows are what they are, "through sickness and health," and more importantly "for better or worse" because every marriage will get worse; ups and downs are inevitable. But it's the groundwork you lay down when it's "better" that will make all the difference during those times when it's worse. Of course, beautiful things can happen in the dark moments. Personally, my most significant growth came in the midst of our worst moments, because of how Hal loved me unconditionally. I have been able to support Hal in ways I never thought I could and love him in ways I didn't think I'd be strong enough to. When life really tried to break us, we made conscious decisions to turn towards each other, instead of away from each other. Brandy and Lance were huge guides to me in those moments of struggle, they knew what it felt like to come to breaking points and knew how to break through those moments, rather than becoming broken. This book is very exciting for me, because of the amazing things it will do for so many. My wish for everyone who reads this book is to know that you are not alone, that we too have gone through the struggle and hurt, but have faith that no matter how bad it is, YOU can make it better. You can make your relationship legendary, and Brandy and Lance

will show you how.

It is our pleasure to introduce to you, our friends, Lance and Brandy Salazar.

With love and gratitude,

- Hal & Ursula Elrod

A NOTE FROM LANCE

"I learned that courage was not the absence of fear, but the triumph over it. The brave man is not he who does not feel afraid, but he who conquers that fear."

—NELSON MANDELA, anti-apartheid revolutionary, political leader, and philanthropist

How important is The Miracle Morning to our marriage? For starters, it was one of the catalysts to saving it. This is because it had a lot to do with saving *me*.

Let me explain.

In 2014, Brandy and I almost divorced. She asked me to move out. While I was crushed, I knew the request was coming. It wasn't the first time we considered splitting up, but this was the time it seemed incredibly real. This time, we discussed who would get what, how we would divide time with the girls, and where I would move.

I was heartbroken for our marriage. I loved Brandy, but I didn't love *us*. Truthfully, I didn't love *me* anymore either. I was depressed, lacked confidence and purpose, and felt I had lost a sense of who I was. For a long time, I blamed Brandy for this. I was jealous of her business success, jealous of her constant networking with creative entrepreneurs, and jealous of her personal growth.

Our story is pretty common. We got married in 2005 and lived that blissful, we-can-do-anything-we-want, newlywed life. We could take weekend trips whenever we wanted.

"Do you want to go wine-tasting this afternoon?" one of us would ask. "Absolutely! Let's drop everything and go!" the other would reply.

There wasn't much real responsibility in our marriage until that one, crazy, life-altering event that no one prepares you for: PARENTHOOD.

Becoming parents —becoming a dad— changed everything. But mostly, it changed our relationship. We were *not* prepared. Becoming a dad further exposed me to all my faults. It exposed all my programming in which I lacked any form of emotional intelligence.

Like many other couples, we deprioritzed our marriage; we became disconnected, and the sole focus was on the newborn child. We put little to no effort into our relationship, and thus began the unraveling of our marriage. And then we decided to have another kid. This only made matters worse for our relationship.

Before 2014, things weren't always bad. There were good times, but our marriage lacked a vision. I lived with defeatist thoughts. Any time things were "going well," I would always wonder when they were going to be bad again. I never thought that the happy moments would stick around for very long.

The problem was that we were caught in this cycle of only fixing what was broken, **instead of creating a marriage we desired**. This wasn't the marriage we wanted for ourselves, and it certainly wasn't the marriage we wanted for our daughters one day either.

Deep inside, I knew I could be a better husband, a better father, and a better man. While I felt stuck, I was also fed up with the direction I had been heading.

But I was also afraid. I was afraid of the unknown. I was afraid of change. I was afraid of my wife rejecting me further. I was afraid of what others thought of me. But fear also got me to this place in my marriage where I wasn't happy. I knew something had to change.

You'll hear Brandy's side of this journey, but I know that a lot changed when she was convinced by a couple of super-successful entrepreneur friends/coaches to not give up on our marriage. I think they kicked her butt and helped her see her own DNA on the matter. These two amazing people influenced us to stick it out, at least to give it one last try before calling it quits.

Brandy and I came to an agreement that we have termed "putting our marriage on the shelf." This meant that we would stay together but remove all obligations and pressure of intimacy and connection. We would do what we needed to take care of the house and our environment **while getting to work on ourselves.** We would let go of any expectations of how this self-work would impact our marriage. We would just "see how it goes." You'll hear about our Four Legendary Relationship Elements in this book—and this work I'm speaking of is that of the You Element.

For me, this meant embarking on a personal growth journey, something I had never done before. I needed to get myself back. While I could tell a huge story here, I'll share with you what set all this growth in motion…what kicked it off.

Brandy was involved in an organization called 1Life Fully Lived. For their upcoming October 2014 conference, they had booked Hal Elrod to be their keynote speaker, and thus the book *The Miracle Morning* was purchased for our home. So that Brandy could familiarize herself with its concepts before the conference, she began her own Miracle Morning routine. I saw how she got up in the morning with intention and purpose. I wanted the same.

It seems funny looking back, how weird it was doing this for the first time. There I was, in my early forties, beginning to "learn" new things about myself and the world around me. In the sections following, I'll share some of my personal favorite Life S.A.V.E.R.S. tools, especially those resources I used and books I read that **radically changed me in a very short period of time.**

Brandy was also speaking at that 1Life Fully Lived conference I mentioned. She was fortunate enough that at the speakers' meeting ahead of the event, she and Hal were the first people in the room. They had a chance to chat and get to know each other. He shared with her that he was hosting his very first event, the Best Year Ever Blueprint and that she should attend. Brandy regretfully expressed that she could not because her sister's baby was due that same weekend but that she would send her husband—*me*—in her place.

The first annual Best Year Ever Blueprint was the very first personal growth event I had ever attended. I knew no one, and I was alone. Yet, understanding the journey I was on, I knew I had to break free of the person I had been for the past several years to blossom into the person I wanted to become. And so I went *all in*. Old Lance would have sat quietly, just watching and taking notes…a wallflower. Not New Lance. New Lance took the bull by the horns and let this experience transform him. To sit here, as I type, and think about going from being "alone" at an event to making friends that I still have today gets me pretty teared up. I am forever grateful.

My life would never be the same. And here we are, from that event to co-authoring this book for you now. It's quite the adventure. Some might call it luck. But I like to think that there was a power much larger than us that brought Hal into our lives.

In thirty short days, I went from being a person my wife wanted nothing to do with to a man that she was attracted to, with whom she wanted to be, with whom she wanted to create the most amazing marriage.

The Miracle Morning has had so much to do with reconnecting us as a couple. We believe in it so much that we created a way for the two of us to practice it together. Since it's had the power to help save our marriage, I know it has the power to impact your relationship in magical and legendary ways, no matter where you are in your journey with your partner right now.

~ Lance

A NOTE FROM BRANDY

"You either SUCK, DON'T SUCK,
or you are LEGENDARY."

—CHRISTOPHER LOCHHEAD,
legendary author, podcaster, and entrepreneur

I remember the first time I heard Christopher say those words, *they hit me in the gut.* And as I sat there in the auditorium and knew, without a doubt, that if this was the scale, I clearly "didn't suck."

If you were to ask just about anyone who knew me, they would disagree. They would confidently say my life was more along the "legendary" side of that scale. You see, from the outside, I had a life of which most people dream. I ran an eight-figure business with a lot of social accolades, was married to a handsome man who also had a successful career, had two beautiful daughters in private school, and lived in a fancy house in the best neighborhood in town. I am sure you are asking yourself, *how the heck was SHE in the "don't suck" category?*

Well, little did everyone—especially those on social media and in the auditorium with me— know, my marriage was failing, my health was "suck" level, my daughter was having anxiety attacks, and I felt like I couldn't breathe most nights while I attempted to decompress (unless I had wine, which helped to take the edge off).

I sat in the audience that daydreaming about what "legendary" could look like for me. I remember hearing Christopher say, "Who says you can't have it all? Who says you can't have epic health and thriving relationships, live where you want, and have a fulfilling career?" Was he right? What the heck was I doing so wrong?

As I sit here years later, I can now tell you where things had gone sour. To start, according to the scale, my childhood examples of how to "do life" and sustain deep relationships fell right into the "suck" category. So, really, as a girl with two addict parents, who had been a victim of childhood abuse and had no high school diploma, getting myself to "don't suck" was quite the accomplishment.

The truth is, for the most part, my childhood wounds fuel me. I know with every fiber of my being that what I went through wasn't for nothing. The insanity I experienced gifted me a lot of great tools that you can't learn in school: courage, grit, perseverance, problem-solving, leadership, sales skills, empathy, and so on. But it also gifted me a strong desire for external validation and a desperation to be accepted by people who appeared successful.

I turned as far away from being like my family as I possibly could. For better or worse, that included not speaking to them. In doing so, my one-dimensional belief of success caused me to sacrifice my relationship with the new family I worked so hard to get, the one I had always wanted. And, even worse, I sacrificed myself.

Success is an interesting thing. I was never taught to define it for myself or truly grasp that it meant more than making a lot of money and getting social acceptance.

My desire to be "successful" outweighed my desire for a deeply connected relationship with my husband and daughters, partially because I didn't know what was truly possible and partially because that would have taken me risking some of my external success to invest the time it would take. Additionally, my husband and daughters didn't give me the validation that the rest of the world did when I accomplished something awesome. In fact, to the contrary, they had a way of pushing my buttons. You know, those areas of weakness—those triggers—that take you right back to the dark corners of yourself. Yep, they do that instead.

So, from the moment I sat in that auditorium seeing and feeling what my days would look like if I designed my own legendary life, everything began to change.

Dismantling my life was not easy and did not go off without its own set of struggles, but through this process, I began to truly know what my priorities were and to gain the courage to live a life I designed. Over the next few years, I deconstructed and completely rebuilt my life. And I am still doing it.

Today, as I sit here, I can proudly say that my life is legendary, especially when it comes to my marriage.

This doesn't mean my life is perfect. I am not a fan of that word, anyway. When my life looked the most perfect, I "didn't suck." Today, my life is peaceful, and I am freer than I have ever felt and more in love with my husband than I have ever been. We've freed our daughter from anxiety and "Life School" both of the girls from home (hard to be a "Life School" graduate and not teach the humans I birthed those skills as well, right?). I am in better health than I was at our wedding—which is saying a lot because let's be honest, I worked my tail off for those perfect pictures.

So, how did I get from "don't suck" to "legendary?"

It was an evolution. I had some major problems to unwind: relationships that weren't healthy, beliefs that held me back, and some major self-love issues (clearly). But the steps were simple.

- I worked hard to get clear on what I desired, what my priorities truly were.

- I got clear on who I needed to become to make that life a reality and changed the conversations I was having with myself and others accordingly.

- I identified the steps to get there.

- I found coaches, teachers, friends, and resources to help me.

- And with unwavering faith (learned from Hal Elrod), I put one foot in front of the other.

- I would then simply check in, go back to step one, adjust my sail, and start again.

My biggest adjustment was prompted by a serious and vulnerable conversation with my dear friend Beverly Steiner. The conversation was intended to discuss a women's mastermind group, but she had a strong desire for it to be co-ed. I was at the point of filing for divorce from Lance, so I clearly wasn't interested in a co-ed mastermind group. I was very honest about it, and her response was simply, "So I guess we are not here to discuss the mastermind after all." Sometimes life's greatest gifts come when you least expect it.

My friend had been divorced from a good man, her children were grown, and she had a very real and blunt perspective of regret. All the questions she had for me about what was dividing Lance and I were met with a similar answer each time: that we had lost connection and were no longer in love.

My husband is a great man, we have two young daughters together, we are both honest and hard-working people, and, at the time, we were trying the best we could with the tools we had.

Were we really about to split custody of our daughters, battle our finances, and unravel everything we had put into this relationship because we lost connection? The reality was that we hadn't given our relationship the energy and time it needed or deserved.

As I sat across from my beautiful friend, who gave me the most loving yet ass-kicking advice of my life, I knew what I had to do. I had to go home and fix this.

Either I needed to leave my husband or invite him on the journey and do the work it would take to create a legendary relationship. Because, at this point, legendary is what I'm aiming for, right?

Well, as chance should have it, one of the resources that came my way just happened to be (drum roll!) *The Miracle Morning*. Truth is, there aren't many resources out there that can impact your life as much, and as quickly, as this one. However (and more importantly for my journey and this part of the story), I collected another resource during that process: a friend in Hal Elrod. I was blessed to meet him at an event shortly after my Miracle Morning success, and anyone who knows him knows why he goes by "Yo' Pal Hal." He is one of the kindest, most inspiring and giving people you will ever meet!

Which leads us to take you along on the journey that we took to create what we have today. Just like the original *Miracle Morning* book, we will show you how to begin a journey to becoming a legendary couple, one morning at a time.

~ Brandy

INTRODUCTION

"The grass is greener where you water it."

—NEIL BARRINGHAM, author and mental health advocate

No matter what source you read, data confirms that the divorce trend has stayed steady at around 50 percent.

When we dove into the research of relationship fulfillment, we wanted to know: *how bad is it, really?* How many of the remaining 50 percent who stayed married were actually happy in their relationships?

In his book, *You Can Be Right (or You Can Be Married)*, Dana Adam Shapiro suggests that only 17 percent of marriages are happy. "Fifty percent of marriages end, and of marriages that stay together, I think a third are happy, a third are happy enough, and a third are unhappy." It sounds a lot like the scale Christopher Lochhead proposes about, well, anything you do in life, "you either suck, don't suck, or are legendary."

So, how do those of us *not* in the "17 Percent Happy Club" get in? How do we gain membership to something that seems so exclusive and so elusive?

If someone had sat us down and explained what our odds of success were, we would have clearly made a different choice. Not to say we wouldn't have gotten married, but we sure would have taken a different approach in the early stages of matrimony. We would have been more proactive, preventative, and strategic. But we didn't, and we weren't. We had no clue that marriage could be as complicated as it was, especially after having kids. We quickly became one of the "unhappy/suck" couples and stayed there for years.

Our marriage became an endless roller coaster of connection and disconnection. A consistent cycle of liking each other followed by not wanting to spend a single minute together. We would go through phases of fixing what was broken and feeling a smidgen of confidence, followed by an obstacle that would derail us completely. Some disagreements could cause us to totally unravel and go months without feeling connected. In those times, we were consistently fighting, from the big things to the little things. Brandy was the master at being snappy and picking fights, while Lance would get overwhelmed and completely shut down, stonewalling Brandy.

When we would "try" in our marriage, we sure weren't trying the right things or taking the right approach.

Sadly, this rollercoaster is common, and there are a lot of reasons why couples get to a place of disconnection and disengagement. If you read couples' surveys, they often cite the same symptoms: lack of communication, lack of common interests, little to no sex, fighting about money or kids, feeling bored, etc. But here's what's crazy about this: if couples can clearly say *what* is negatively impacting their relationships, then why is it so hard to figure out *how* to get to that place of a thriving and flourishing connection?

We had been through counseling, we had read the books, yet we couldn't seem to get our marriage together. We couldn't get along. But we also wanted to find the answer to the question.

With our backs against the wall, on the verge of telling our daughters we would be getting a divorce, we made a different choice. We decided to give it one last chance.

After that fateful discussion with her dear friend Bev, Brandy walked through the door of our house, right up to Lance and said, "Not only are we *not* going to get divorced, but we are going to make the most amazing marriage we possibly can!"

This was when everything changed. We knew that what we had done in the past hadn't yielded the results we wanted.

With nothing to lose and everything to gain, we started with the simple yet powerful question:

What would our relationship look like if it were *legendary*?

What if we took other areas where we had experienced success and applied it to our relationship? Brandy had certainly thrived in business, forging successful systems with teams of people. Lance was fantastic with health, using goals, plans, and milestones to run dozens of half marathons and marathons.

What if we took the most effective tools and philosophies used by successful business and health experts, added in proven positive psychology methods, and applied these concepts to our relationship? How could we use them and simply ask different questions along the way?

And if our mission was to create this legendary relationship, then we knew we had to do something radically different to make this happen. We were ready to take control and design the best possible relationship we could. We were done falling into the same traps.

---

leg·end·ar·y
lejən derē/
adjective
remarkable, esteemed, honored,
well-known, storied

A legendary relationship for us was feeling madly in love, having fun together, laughing a lot, feeling like we could safely talk about anything, feeling free to be ourselves, and enjoying a great sex life.

Becoming legendary surely wasn't an easy task, but the obsessive dedication of doing the right things quickly yielded promising results.

Within thirty days, we knew there was something to fight for, and we began to fall in love again.

We have gone from one extreme of almost divorcing to the other extreme of being madly in love. Our relationship is now on fire. Things are now clicking. And in the moments when things aren't clicking, we've developed the emotional intelligence and harnessed the relationship skills to get it clicking again.

We have continued to study relationships and success. We read a lot of books (like, *a lot*) and have become quite obsessed with implementing tools and resources through the lens of relationship improvement. We try anything and everything. We have become relationship guinea pigs. We extensively examine the things that are working for us because we want to both understand the "why" behind them and challenge our beliefs in what makes them work. We wanted to study the science of it all. Is this something that could work only for us, or was this something that could work for other people?

One tool we utilized was undoubtedly beneficial for our marriage, for ourselves, and for our life together. At this point, it would be crazy if we didn't share what we've learned with other couples. The research and the "why" are all in this book, and we know that if the steps are followed, it will make a difference in your relationship. That resource is Hal Elrod's *The Miracle Morning*.

OUR DESIRE FOR THIS BOOK:

The Miracle Morning for Couples gives you the simple framework for your relationship vision, while helping you create and maintain that vision in a simple routine you can do each morning.

Books that claim to change/grow/help your relationship are a dime a dozen, and there are a lot of great and legendary publications out there. But what this book does is provide a path for you to design and plan for your intimate relationship. It helps you create that model, construct that vision, and change your behavior, so you can build what you want through the foundation of a morning routine.

It helps you begin the chrysalis phase of your relationship, one that can lead to the eventual emergence of a butterfly.

We hope this book is a catalyst to transforming hundreds of thousands of intimate relationships, but if it simply changes *yours*, then the effort spent writing these words and telling our stories was worth every moment.

Consider this your invitation to shake things up, get a little uncomfortable, and experience The Miracle Morning for Couples.

OVERVIEW

*"Long ago, I realized that success leaves clues and that
people who produce outstanding results do specific things to
create those results. I believed that if I precisely duplicated the
actions of others, I could reproduce the same quality of results
that they had."*

—TONY ROBBINS, author, entrepreneur, philanthropist, and life
coach

Now that we know most relationships either end in divorce or
remain in an unhappy union, let's look at some of the foundational
problems to blame. We have found that the emotional relationship
rollercoaster that leads to lack of communication, lack of intimacy,
increased fighting about money and kids, etc., is generally caused by
one or all the following three common offenders.

Lack of Direction

To have success in anything, you must know where you are going
and how you will get there. Many couples don't realize that they have
the power and freedom to design their own relationship.

"You mean we can create a plan—a blueprint—for our relationship?" they wonder.

Think about it. If you wanted to lose ten pounds, what would you do? You consider the ten-pound victory as the vision and reverse engineer it. You would create a plan—decide what you would do to lose ten pounds (like running, eating well, and working out) and commit to when you would do your weight-loss activities (in the morning, evening, etc.); take massive action on that plan (actually doing what you said you would do and when); and then track your progress. You might even change some things in your plan if you aren't on target for your goals.

Well, we're here to tell you that you can do exactly this for your relationship. The two of you can create that vision for what your amazing relationship can look like and create a plan to make it a reality.

Little Time Invested

Plain and simple, if you want a legendary relationship, you must put in the time to create it. Couples that are dissatisfied with their relationship don't put in the time and energy needed to create the connection they desire. They might *say* that their relationship is a top priority, but their actions tell a different story. They end up too busy, giving most of their energy to other life areas. For example, they might bury themselves in their business or work, hoping to achieve complete fulfillment from this external success. Or, they might make the kids the center of the family universe, remaining constantly busy shuffling them to and from school, friends' houses, and extracurricular activities. Although career and business success are important, and kids' schedules and needs take a lot of attention, giving these areas all your best time causes most couples to feel disconnected and dissatisfied in their relationships.

It takes "putting your money where your mouth is" to make your relationship a priority. Make time, be 100 percent present when you are together, schedule dates, create boundaries with your business and your kids, say no to unimportant requests…in other words, make your relationship with each other a top priority.

Loss of Self

When you first started dating, you each had your own life. You both stood on your own two feet. Somewhere along the way, it is common for one or both partners to lose their sense of self, becoming so caught up in the "to do's" of life that they forget who they are, what they love, and what they stand for.

We want to make something clear: while we believe that you can create an amazing life with another person (your partner), it's false to think that you need someone else to make you happy. This is a very difficult concept for couples to understand. We've been conditioned to believe that finding that "soulmate" is what we need to have fulfillment in life. We've been told that we need to *search* for that happiness, especially from someone else.

Fairy tales and the idea of Prince Charming, the Princess, and "Happily Ever After" have been sold to us all since childhood. And Hollywood keeps that fire stoked. We latch on to the image of Tom Cruise in *Jerry Maguire* yearning in a state of desperation that "You. Complete. Me." Or that moment when John Cusack's character stands outside his love interest's window with a boombox in some grand act of love. Or just watch any movie based on books written by Nicholas Sparks. We believe this is what we need to feel love. Harboring this ideal leads to a slippery slope of blame, loss of self, and feelings of inadequacy when we sail in troubled waters and things aren't going smoothly.

These assumptions guide you down a path of codependency and foster the expectation that your partner must make you happy for you to feel satisfied or content. If codependency is not solved, your relationship can be doomed.

We are here to tell you that you are a whole and complete person on your own. Your partner does not complete you or make you whole. You can be in the relationship consistently working on yourself, but you are not "incomplete." Your partner is not your "other half" or, even worse, "your better half" (as you hear people say all the time). You create your own happiness. You create your own peace. Your partner is not responsible for your happiness or your peacefulness.

Blaming them for any deficiency or feeling of dissatisfaction in your life is senseless. Further, your partner can't *make* you happy or sad even if they want to. Your state of mind is all on you. Pointing your finger at your partner when you're feeling unhappy is rooted in a defeatist mindset. You're basically saying that it's his or her fault that I am feeling this way, meaning I have no power to fix it. I do not have any control. But the only person you *do* have control over is you.

You can pick someone to share yourself with and create a magical, purposeful, and meaningful life together. That connection and sharing of love and life can be one of the most amazing experiences we can ever have for ourselves. But you need to bring your whole self, your best self, your constantly-learning-and-growing self, your emotionally intelligent self to the relationship for it to grow and prosper. And you need to love yourself *first*.

When you do that, you can build interdependence in your relationship, which is different from codependence. Let's explain it this way:

Imagine two people about to go backpacking. If one person is carrying both packs, all the stuff, because the other person can't bear any of the weight, that trip isn't going to get very far and will probably fail. This is codependence. But, if they each carry their own packs, their own stuff, and maybe a few shared items in their packs, they can have an amazing adventure together. This is interdependence.

Interdependence is the ability to collaborate and be intertwined with another. It can amplify the best parts of each of you in life together. It is exponential, greater than the sum of its parts. Creating interdependence for your relationship is one of the primary goals of this book.

So, how do we solve for this? How do we understand and accept that we create our own happiness? How do we make the distinction between blaming someone else for not making us happy and taking the responsibility that we must create it for ourselves? How do we go from the place of feeling like a victim to the feeling of empowerment?

While it may seem paradoxical, your independence, your own personal growth, and your own self-care need to be in harmony with your desire to grow together as a couple. You were two whole people before you came together, and you remain two whole people in the relationship. When a person shows up in their intimate relationship, takes responsibility for setting the tone for himself or herself, and takes the lead for their own life with love and integrity, both they and their partner have the greatest opportunity to experience what they both most deeply desire.

Don't worry, we will tackle all three of these pitfalls that may be holding the two of you back from having the most amazing connection possible.

Let's start with . . .

WHAT WE DID

We logically knew that the first step to a legendary relationship was becoming two legendary people...two whole, happy, healthy, confident people. We also knew that to be "legendary" together, we needed to have fun with each other, feel like we were "in love" again, and have more connected and more frequent intimacy. These were the things we desired for our marriage.

So we sat down and talked about when our relationship was at its best. It wasn't always bad. We clearly enjoyed being together enough to get married. What did we enjoy about each other, about being together? We knew the answers could help create our goals! What did we truly desire in our relationship? What would a legendary relationship look like for us?

As any successful couple would do, we grabbed Post-it® notes (a lot of them!) and Sharpies. And we began to put these ideas up on our sliding glass door. At first, it looked like little bits of paper had exploded all over the glass.

We began organizing the ideas we wrote on those Post-it® notes into nameless categories, which helped us to see some themes. Stepping back, seeing our desires and success clues together, right in front of our faces, made it very clear that we had *four big areas* in our marriage to work and focus on.

Having that framework finally gave us hope and some clearer direction. We knew if we could develop these four areas, commit, create a vision, and see it through to completion, we couldn't fail.

THE FOUR LEGENDARY RELATIONSHIP ELEMENTS

The Four Legendary Relationship Elements are YOU, PART-NERS, FRIENDS, and LOVERS, in this order. The fundamental belief is that each one of these four elements must be nurtured to create a deep and meaningful connection with your partner. Specifically, one is foundational to the others and must be stable and thriving for the next one to be successfully developed. As you can see in the pyramid below, the foundation is built with You—two happy and healthy individuals. From there, the Partners Element can be cultivated. This is where the "business" side of your marriage takes place. Having a shared vision and plan on finances, household chores and roles, parenting beliefs and systems, helps free up space, time, and energy toward creating a solid Friendship with your partner. When that Friendship is maximized, and at its best, you can move into the true intimacy part of your relationship as Lovers. Again—each element builds on the others. You can't rest your marriage on the Lovers Element if all the others have not been developed. This creates a house without a strong foundation, putting your relationship at risk.

LEGENDARY RELATIONSHIP ELEMENTS

THE BEGINNING

Do you remember when you fell in love? When you first begin a relationship with another person, the euphoria pushes you very quickly into the Friends and Lovers Elements. You are having fun together, enjoying getting to know each other, spending as much time together as possible. You can't keep our hands off each other. This time of discovery is intoxicating. Hardly a moment goes by when you don't think of each other. When we first fall in love, household roles, parenting, and finances don't even cross our minds. This is all normal. There is a scientific component happening that is out of our control. The natural neurochemical response that happens during the process of courting and falling in love has been called "rose-colored glasses" because of the happy blend of oxytocin and dopamine released. This is a period in which the warm glow of romance minimizes the differences between two people and highlights the similarities. *We are one. We are the same. You are perfect. I am yours, and you are mine.*

THE PARTNERSHIP LOOP

Once we get married—though sometimes not until we have children—we are suddenly thrust into Partnership: scrambling just to survive and keep the kids alive, loosely managing daily tasks, chores, bills…you name it. We feel we have little—if any—time for each other. We begin wishing to return to how the relationship *used* to be, yearning for the past or something new and different than what we have right now. We call this the "Partnership Loop." It is where so many couples get stuck. It was where *we* were stuck. At that point, couples are at significant risk for arguments, power struggles, complacency, and even resentment. It is exactly where we were stalled and almost called it quits.

However, when you build a strong You—with each spouse confident, happy, healthy, growing, and emotionally intelligent—the foundation of the relationship is sound. From there, the Partnership of your marriage is envisioned, redesigned, and reconstructed as an efficient system. And then the two of you reconnect and redevelop a deep and knowing Friendship that leads to the pinnacle of your relationship as Lovers. Intimate, joyful, knowing, sharing, loving, and passionate.

Florence Kaslow, Ph.D., director of the Florida Couple and Family Institute in West Palm Beach and clinical professor at Duke University in Durham, North Carolina, puts it this way: "Each partner's personal development and the normal events of life necessitate continual adaptation, both individually and as a couple."

THE MIRACLE MORNING

The Miracle Morning is a foundational and groundbreaking tool that was the first step we took to create the time, space, and energy needed to radically improve our marriage. It was the first practice we committed to that knocked down the original domino of reconnecting our marriage. It created the stage for us to take massive action on that design and vision we had for our relationship. It should be your first step, too.

And because it was so successful in helping each of us recapture our individuality and our sense of self and purpose, we created new steps and activities at the end of it that we do together as a couple, side by side. These new steps allowed us to stay the course of that vision we created for years to come.

SEPARATENESS and TOGETHERNESS

In their book *Becoming Married*, Herbert Anderson and Robert Cotton Fite talk about having a "room of one's own." This concept is not about a physical space (although it can be) as much as an emotional space. It refers to the delicate balance between needing connection within a relationship and the need to still be an individual with autonomy and uniqueness. A "room of one's own" honors the need to be separate at times where one can examine one's thoughts, feelings, and wishes while realizing the need to also be committed to the relationship. There is a paradox in the "separate but together" aspect of a relationship. Couples often negotiate the balance between separateness and togetherness in an ongoing dynamic requiring delicate conversation and cooperation. It is most difficult when two people's needs do not match at the time, or where one person needs more space, and another might need more connection. Like many aspects of a relationship, it requires open communication, the ability to safely express one's needs, and the ability to know what one is feeling. Additionally, it often involves compromise. It is an important aspect to consider in premarital work but will usually need renegotiating, even when couples have been together for a length of time. Different stages of life may present new challenges to the established balance.

The spirit of The Miracle Morning for Couples rests on the principle of separateness and togetherness.

Viewing relationships through the lens of separateness and togetherness (meaning it's OK for you to be yourself, be able to influence your partner lovingly, and create a life-journey side-by-side) gives hope even in the midst of hardship, relieves some of the anxiety when the two of you are not happy at the moment, and gives you an agenda for working through challenges.

We passionately believe that each person in the relationship should be growing and improving each day (which is why we love Hal's Life S.A.V.E.R.S. so much!). Clearly, each of you can explore different areas of interest to your personal development but growing and evolving is non-negotiable for both of you. To create the legendary relationship you truly desire, you need to bring your best self to the table. We'd like to think you agree, or you probably wouldn't be reading the book in your hands.

HOW TO USE THIS BOOK

The book is made up of four sections:

Section 1 & 2 — YOU: We will walk you through the Life S.A.V.E.R.S. and the You Element, helping you design your "room of one's own," standing on your own two feet so that you can create the happiest and healthiest You for your relationship.

Section 3 — TOGETHER: We will introduce T.E.A.M. and the extension of your Miracle Morning routine, showcasing the other three Elements: Partners, Friends, and Lovers, and helping you forge a morning routine the two of you can practice together, side by side, to foster a lasting connection.

Section 4 — BECOMING LEGENDARY: Here, we will help you put it all together, beyond just the morning routine, so that the two of you can take massive action on creating the relationship you desire.

By incorporating *The Miracle Morning for Couples* into your lives together, you can create rhythms, stimulate continual growth, promote adaptability where needed, and strengthen your Four Relationship Elements one day at a time.

SECTION I:

YOU AND THE MIRACLE MORNING

— 1 —
WHY MORNINGS MATTER
TO YOUR RELATIONSHIP
(MORE THAN YOU THINK)

"'Life's too short' is repeated often enough to be a cliché,
but this time it's true. You don't have
enough time to be both unhappy and mediocre.
It's not just pointless; it's painful."

—SETH GODIN, New York Times bestselling author

"You've got to wake up every morning with determination
if you're going to go to bed with satisfaction."

—GEORGE LORIMER, American journalist and author

In some ways, Lance has always been a morning person. He's always been able to get up early if he needed to; most of his twenties were spent working in hospitals, with shifts commonly starting at five or six a.m. But he was getting up early out of *necessity*; it wasn't joyful. It wasn't with motivation. It was always a struggle. There were even times when he would get up early to go for runs so that he could get it over with. But here's where he had it all wrong: he wasn't "friends" with his mornings. He wasn't getting up excited. Even when he was training for a race, he felt more like a suffering martyr than a conquering hero.

What's more, there was even a selfish motive for his early rising. He did it to "get away" … not to grow, at least not as a person on the path to becoming his best self. What's changed today is that he has more purpose, more "why" for the reason he gets up before the sun does. He now wants to grow for himself, for his wife, and for his family.

Focusing on the intention of *why* he was getting up early was what mattered. Getting to this place with his mornings has meant the difference. It meant the difference between staying together with Brandy or getting divorced.

How you start each morning sets your mindset, and the context, for the rest of your day. Start every day with a purposeful, disciplined, growth-infused, and goal-oriented morning, and you're virtually guaranteed to crush your day.

Do you start your day feeling overwhelmed? I'd be willing to bet that most couples do. In fact, it can be an incredible challenge just to set an alarm clock. Their day starts with feeling overwhelmed about their life and their relationship, and they often feel unable to tackle their other priorities. They have no idea where to start and how to fix or move their relationship forward in a positive direction.

But what if you could have that hour of peace and quiet for you and your significant other you've been dreaming about? What if you could reclaim some time together so that communication could be improved, and you could talk about what matters most? If you could grasp that clean, uncluttered mental space where the two of you could regain your sense of elegance and dignity, where you're in total control and can proceed in an orderly, self-nurturing, yet connecting fashion? But you know you can't, or maybe you can, but not today. Maybe when you get all of your other life priorities sorted out.

It's no wonder most couples start their days with procrastination, letting mediocrity and complacency set the agenda, along with sending a message to their subconscious that says they don't have enough energy or even the will to get out of bed. They think today will be another free-for-all where their personal goals go out the window.

Add to this the fact that most people believe they aren't early risers, and the pattern of procrastination shows up early in life.

But what if you could change it?

What if, when the alarm clock starts beeping in the morning, you could consider it to be *life's first gift*? It's the gift of time that you can dedicate to becoming the person you need to be to achieve all your goals and dreams—for yourself and your relationship—while the rest of the world (or your kid(s)) is still asleep.

You might be thinking, *all of this sounds great, guys. But. I. Am. Not. A. Morning. Person.*

We understand. We really do! You're not saying anything we haven't told ourselves a thousand times before. And believe us, we tried—and failed—many times to take control of our mornings. But that was before we discovered *The Miracle Morning*.

Stay with us here. We know you want to reconnect with your partner, but we bet you also want to stop arguing—about money challenges, or the best way to raise the kids—and release the intense and not-so-great emotions that go along with those challenges. These things get in the way of creating a relationship that thrives because they affect your self-esteem and prevent you from feeling good about yourself and your life.

We are firm believers in the advice given at the start of every airplane flight: put your oxygen mask on first, and then help others. You won't be able to help anyone if you pass out due to lack of oxygen. Therefore, building and creating an excellent You Element is vital to your relationship's success.

Many couples don't see this simple truth. They think that success means putting your own needs last, and they have so much to do that they never get to those personal needs. Over time, they end up exhausted, depressed, resentful, and overwhelmed. They forget about the absolute necessity of self-care.

Sound familiar?

Then know this:

Mornings are the key to all of it.

More important than even the *time* that you start your day is the *mindset* with which you start your day.

Although there's a chance you're reading this book after months or years of being disconnected from your partner, there's also a good chance that you're reading this book in the early stages of your personal growth journey, which means that you may be feeling overwhelmed and looking for answers. If that's the case, then learning to practice your Miracle Morning before anything else is important to make sure you get uninterrupted time. The good news is that it's worth it, and it is far more fun and rewarding than you might expect.

But before we get into exactly *how* you can master your mornings alone and together, let me make the case for *why*. Because, believe us, once you've uncovered the profound truth about mornings, you'll never want to miss one again.

Why Mornings Matter So Much

The more you explore the power of early rising and morning rituals, the more proof mounts that the early bird gets *a lot* more than the worm. Following are just a few of the key advantages you're about to learn how to experience for yourself.

You'll be more proactive and productive in your relationship. Christoph Randler is a professor of biology at the University of Education in Heidelberg, Germany. In the July 2010 issue of *Harvard Business Review***, Randler found that "People whose performance peaks in the morning are better positioned for career success because they're more proactive than people who are at their best in the evening." According to** *New York Times* **bestselling author and world-renowned entrepreneur Robin Sharma, "If you study many of the most productive people in the world, they all had one thing in common—they were early risers."**

You'll anticipate problems between the two of you and head them off at the pass. Randler went on to surmise that morning people hold all of the important cards. They are "better able to anticipate and minimize problems, are proactive, have greater professional success and ultimately make higher wages." He noted that morning people are able to anticipate problems and handle them with grace and ease. If you think about it, this could be the key to decreasing the level of stress that inevitably comes with adding little ones to your household.

You'll plan like a pro. Planning is very important to create a relationship and a life that thrives and flourishes. It's been said that *when we fail to plan, we are indirectly planning to fail.* Morning folks have the time to organize, anticipate, and prepare for their day. Our sleepy counterparts are reactive, leaving a lot to chance. Aren't you more stressed when you sleep through your alarm? Getting up with the sun (or before) lets you jump-start your day. While everyone else is running around trying (and failing) to get their day under control, you'll be more calm, cool, and collected. Plus, your partner and family will appreciate it.

You'll have more energy. One component of your new Miracle Mornings will be exercise, which often is something that gets neglected when you think you're too busy. Yet, in as little as a few minutes, exercise sets a positive tone for the day. Increased blood to the brain will help you think more clearly and focus on what's most important. Fresh oxygen will permeate every cell in your body and increase your energy, which is why when you exercise, you are in a better mood and in better shape, get better sleep, have better sex, and become more productive.

You'll gain early bird attitude advantages. Recently, researchers at the University of Barcelona in Spain compared morning people—those early birds who like to get up at dawn—with evening people—night owls who prefer to stay up late and sleep in. Among the differences, they found that morning people tend to be more persistent and resistant to fatigue, frustration, and difficulties. That translates into not only lower levels of anxiety, decreased rates of depression, and less likelihood of substance abuse, but higher life satisfaction. Sounds good to me! A better attitude has helped us create a more powerful mindset, which has made us a better couple and has helped us be more deeply connected on a level we never thought possible.

The evidence is in, and the experts have had their say. *Mornings contain the secret to an extraordinarily successful life.*

Mornings? Really?

We admit it. To go from *I'm not a morning person* to *I really want to become a morning person* to *I'm up early every morning, and it feels amazing!* is a process. But after some trial and error, you will discover how to outfox, preempt, and foil your inner late sleeper so you can make early rising a habit. Plus, you'll have a built-in accountability partner to motivate and encourage you. Okay, sounds great in theory, but you might be shaking your head and telling yourself, *There's no way. I'm already cramming twenty-seven hours of stuff into twenty-four-hour days. How on earth could I get up an hour earlier than I already do?*

We ask the question, "How can you not?"

The key thing to understand is that The Miracle Morning isn't about denying yourself another hour of sleep, so you can have an even longer, harder day. It's not even about waking up earlier. It's about waking up *better*.

Hundreds of thousands of people around the planet are already living their own Miracle Mornings. Many of them were night owls. But they're making it work. In fact, they're *thriving*. And it's not because they simply added that extra time to their day. It's because they added *the right* time to their day. And so can the two of you.

Still skeptical? Then let me tell you this: *the hardest part about getting up earlier is the first five minutes.* That's the crucial time when, tucked into your warm bed, you make the decision to start your day or hit the snooze button *just one more time.* It's the moment of truth, and the decision you make right then will change your day, your success, your relationship, and your life.

And that's why the first five minutes is the starting point for *The Miracle Morning for Couples*. It's time for the two of you to win every morning, together! When we win our mornings, we win the day, and we win back our connection with our partner.

In the next chapters, we'll make waking up early easier and more exciting than it's ever been in your life. Even if you've *never* considered yourself to be a morning person, we will show you how to maximize those newfound morning minutes with the Life S.A.V.E.R.S.—the six most powerful, proven personal development practices known to man—for each of you. In the next section, T.E.A.M., we'll cover the four practices that will help you create the most legendary relationship possible.

We will also reveal the principles to maximizing You, as related to accelerating your personal growth and your growth together (Partners, Friends, and Lovers), discuss why you need to structure your life to gain endless amounts of energy, and share how to optimize your ability to stay focused on your goals and what matters most to your relationship.

Finally, we'll cover the critical skills to put it all together, so you can become a legendary couple. There's even a final bonus chapter from Hal that we think you are going to love!

We have a lot of ground to cover in this book, so let's jump right in.

— 2 —
IT ONLY TAKES FIVE MINUTES TO BECOME A MORNING PERSON

"If you really think about it, hitting the snooze
button in the morning doesn't even make sense.
It's like saying, 'I hate getting up in the morning,
so I do it over, and over, and over again.'"

—DEMETRI MARTIN, stand-up comedian

Have you ever considered that how we start our day could be the single most important factor in determining how we live our lives or set our relationship up for success? When we wake up with excitement and create a purposeful, powerful, productive morning, we set ourselves up to win the day.

Yet, most people start their day with resistance and procrastination, hitting the snooze button and waiting until the last possible moment to pry themselves out from beneath their cozy covers. While it may not be obvious, this seemingly innocent act may be sending a detrimental message to our subconscious, programming our psyche with the unconscious belief that we don't have the self-discipline to get out of bed in the morning, let alone do what's necessary to achieve everything else we want for our lives.

Could it be that how we wake up in the morning is impacting who we're becoming, and thus impacting every area of our lives?

When the alarm clock starts beeping in the morning, consider that as life's first *gift*, *challenge*, and *opportunity* to us—all three at the same time—each day. It's the gift of another day, the challenge of making the disciplined decision to get out of bed, and the opportunity to invest time into our personal development so each of us can become the person we need to be to create the life and connection that we truly want with our partner.

The good news is that it is possible to love waking up—and do it easily each day—even if you've *never* been a morning person.

We know you might not believe it. Right now, you might think *that might be true for early birds, but trust me, I've tried. I'm just not a morning person.*

But it is true. We know because we've been there. We used to sleep until the last possible moment when we absolutely had to wake up. And even then, it took us a while to get out of bed. We dreaded mornings. We hated waking up.

And now we love it.

How did we do it? When people ask us how we transformed ourselves into morning people—and transformed our relationship in the process—we tell them we did it in five simple steps, one at a time. We know it may seem downright impossible, but you can do this. And you can do it the same way we did.

That's the critical message about waking up: it's possible to change. Morning people aren't born—they're self-made. You can do it, and it doesn't require the willpower of an Olympic marathoner. We contend that when early rising becomes not only something you do but *who you are*, you will truly love mornings. Waking up will become for you like it is for us: effortless.

Not convinced? Suspend your disbelief a little and let us introduce you to the five-step process that changed our lives. Five simple, snooze-proof keys that made waking up in the morning—even early in the morning—easier than ever before. Without this strategy, we would still be sleeping (or snoozing) through the alarm(s) each morning. Worse, we would still be clinging to the limiting belief that we are not morning people.

And we would have missed a whole world of opportunity to create the deepest connection possible between the two of us.

The Challenge with Waking Up

Waking up earlier is a bit like running: you think you're not a runner—maybe you even *hate* running—until you lace up a pair of running shoes and reluctantly head out the front door at a pace that suggests you might be about to go for a run. With a commitment to overcome your seemingly insurmountable loathing for running, you put one foot in front of the other. Do this for a few weeks, and one day it hits you: *I've become a runner.*

Similarly, if you've resisted waking up in the morning and choosing to hit the *procrastination*—oops, we mean *snooze*—button, then of course you're not *yet* a morning person. But follow the simple step-by-step process that you're about to discover, and when you wake up in a few weeks (maybe even a few days), it will hit you: *OMG, I can't believe it...I've become a morning person!*

However, right now, you might be feeling motivated, excited, optimistic. But what happens tomorrow morning when that alarm goes off? How motivated will you be when you're yanked out of deep sleep in your warm bed by a screaming alarm clock beckoning you into a cold house?

We all know where motivation will be right then. It will be flushed down the toilet and replaced by rationalization. And rationalization is a crafty master—in seconds, we can convince ourselves that we need just a few extra minutes.

And the next thing we know, we're scrambling around the house late for work, late for life. Again.

It's a tricky problem. Just when we need our motivation the most—those first few moments of the day—is precisely when we seem to have the least of it.

The solution, then, is to boost that morning motivation and mount a surprise attack on rationalization. That's what the five following steps do for you. Each step in the process is designed to increase what Hal calls your Wake-Up Motivation Level (WUML).

First thing in the morning, you might have a low WUML, meaning you want nothing more than to go back to sleep when your alarm goes off. That's normal. But by using this simple five-step process (that takes about five minutes), you can generate a high WUML, where you're ready to jump up and embrace the day.

The Five-Step Snooze-Proof Wake-Up Strategy

Minute One: Set Your Intentions *Before* Bed

The first key to waking up is to understand this: *your first thought in the morning is usually the same as your last thought before you sleep.* We bet, for example, that you've had nights where you could hardly fall asleep because you were so excited about waking up the next morning. Whether it was when you were a kid on Christmas Eve or the day before you were leaving for a big vacation, as soon as the alarm clock sounded you opened your eyes, ready to jump out of bed and embrace the day. Why? Because the last thought you had about the coming morning—before you fell asleep—was positive.

On the other hand, if your last thought before bed is something like: *Oh gosh, I can't believe I have to get up in six hours—I'm going to be exhausted in the morning*, then your first thought when the alarm clock goes off is likely to be something like, *Oh gosh, it's already been six hours? Nooo...I just want to keep sleeping!* Consider that it is a self-fulfilling prophecy, and you create your own reality.

The first step, then, is to consciously decide—every night, before bed—to actively and mindfully create a positive expectation for the next morning. Think about how you want to show up for yourself and for your partner. What kind of relationship do you desire? Visualize it and affirm it to yourself and to your partner.

For help on this and to get the precise words to say before bed to create your powerful morning intentions, download *The Miracle Morning Bedtime Affirmations* free at www.TMMBook.com.

Minute Two: Move Your Alarm Clock Across the Room

If you haven't already, be sure to move your alarm clock as far away from your bed as possible. This will make it inevitable that you must actually get out of bed and engage your body in movement to start each day. Motion creates energy, so getting out of bed and walking across the room naturally helps you to wake up.

Most people keep their alarm clock next to their bed, within reach. Think about it: if you keep your alarm clock within reach, then you're still in a partial sleep state after the alarm goes off. Your WUML is at its lowest point, which makes it much more difficult to summon up the discipline to get out of bed. In fact, you may turn off the alarm without even realizing it! On more than a few occasions, we've all convinced ourselves that our alarm clock was merely part of the dream we were having. You're not alone on that one, trust us.

By forcing yourself to get out of bed to turn off the alarm clock, you are setting yourself up for early rising success by instantly increasing your WUML.

However, on a scale of one to ten, your WUML may still be hovering around five, and you'll likely be feeling sleepier than not, so the temptation to turn around and crawl back into bed will still be present. To raise that WUML just a little further, try...

Minute Three: Brush Your Teeth

As soon as you've gotten out of bed and turned off your alarm clock, go directly to the bathroom sink to brush your teeth. We know what you may be thinking: *Really? You're telling me that I need to brush my teeth?* Yes. The point is that you're doing mindless activities for the first few minutes and simply giving your body time to wake up.

After turning off your alarm clock, go directly to the bathroom sink to brush your teeth and splash some water on your face. This simple activity will allow for the passing of more time to increase your WUML even further.

Now that your mouth is minty-fresh, it's time to ...

Minute Four: Drink a Full Glass of Water

It's crucial that you hydrate yourself first thing every morning. After six to eight hours without water, you'll be mildly dehydrated, which causes fatigue. Often, when people feel tired—at any time of the day—what they really need is more water, not more sleep.

Start by getting a glass of water (or you can do what we do and fill it up the night before, so it's already there for you in the morning) and drink it as fast as is comfortable for you. Brandy likes hers with a little fresh lemon juice and electrolytes. The objective is to replace the water you were deprived of during the hours you slept. (And hey, the side benefits of morning hydration are enjoying better, younger-looking skin and maintaining a healthy weight. Not bad for a few ounces of water!)

That glass of water should raise your WUML another notch, which will get you to …

Minute Five: Get Dressed in Your Workout Clothes (or Jump in the Shower)

The fifth step has two options. *Option one* is to get dressed in your exercise clothing, so you're ready to leave your bedroom and immediately engage in your Miracle Morning for Couples. You can either lay out your clothes before you go to bed or even sleep in your workout clothes. (Yes, really.) And for couples, the "night before" prep is especially important to help you go straight into your practice. If you have kids, you can make this part of their bedtime ritual, so they build the habit, too. Our daughters are well aware of the "Mommy/Daddy time" we've created for our relationship each morning.

Option two is to jump in the shower, which is a great way to finish off taking your WUML to the point where staying awake is much easier. A lot of people prefer the morning shower because it helps them wake up and gives them a fresh start to the day. The choice is completely yours.

Regardless of which option you choose, by the time you've executed these five simple steps, your WUML should be high enough that it requires very little discipline to stay awake for your Miracle Morning.

If you were to try to make that commitment the moment your alarm clock first went off—while you were at a WUML of nearly zero—it would be a much more difficult decision to make. The five steps let you build momentum so that, within just a few minutes, you're ready to go instead of feeling groggy.

We have never made it through the first five minutes and decided to go back to bed. Once we are up and moving intentionally through the morning, it becomes much easier to continue being purposeful in our relationship throughout the day.

Miracle Morning Bonus Wake-Up Tips

Although this strategy has worked for thousands of people, these five steps are not the only way to make waking up in the morning easier. Here are a few others I've heard from fellow Miracle Morning practitioners:

- *The Miracle Morning Bedtime Affirmations:* if you haven't done this yet, take a moment now to go to www.TMMbook.com and download the re-energizing, intention-setting *Bedtime Affirmations* document for free. Nothing is more effective for ensuring that you will wake up before your alarm than programming your mind to achieve exactly what you want before you fall asleep.

- Set a timer for your bedroom lights: One member of The Miracle Morning Community shared that he sets his bedroom lights on a timer (you can buy an appliance timer online or at your local hardware store). As his alarm goes off, the lights come on in the room. What a great idea! It's a lot easier to fall back asleep when it's dark—having the lights on tells your mind and body that it's time to wake up. (Whether you use a timer or not, be sure to turn your light on right after you turn your alarm off.)

- Set a timer for your bedroom heater: Another member of The Miracle Morning Community says that in the winter, she keeps a bedroom heater on an appliance timer set to go off fifteen minutes before she wakes up. She keeps it cold at night but warm for waking up so she won't be tempted to crawl back under her covers.

- Sunrise simulation alarm clock: these alarm clocks gradually bring more light into your bedroom, beginning thirty or so minutes before you want to get out of bed. The idea is that they wake you more naturally by getting your mind to think the sun is rising. How cool is that? Numerous companies manufacture these.

Feel free to add to or customize the Five-Step Snooze-Proof Wake-Up Strategy, and if you have any tips that you're open to sharing, we'd love to hear them. Please post them in The Miracle Morning Community at www.MyTMMCommunity.com.

Waking up consistently and easily is all about having an effective, predetermined, step-by-step strategy to increase your WUML in the morning. Don't wait to try this! Start tonight by reading *The Miracle Morning Bedtime Affirmations* to set a powerful intention for waking up tomorrow morning, moving your alarm clock across the room, setting a glass of water on your nightstand, and committing to the other two steps for the morning.

Taking Immediate Action

There's no need to wait to get started implementing the power of early rising. As Anthony Robbins has said, "When is NOW a good time for you to do that?" Now, indeed, would be perfect! In fact, the sooner you start, the sooner you'll begin to see results, including increased energy, a better attitude, and, of course, a happier home life and relationship.

Step One: Set your alarm for thirty to sixty minutes earlier than you usually wake up, for the next thirty days. That's it; just thirty to sixty minutes for thirty days, starting now. And be sure to write into your schedule to do your first Miracle Morning… *tomorrow morning.* That's right, don't use *waiting until you finish the book* as an excuse to procrastinate on getting started!

If you're feeling resistant at all, because maybe you've tried to make changes in the past but haven't followed through, here's a suggestion: turn now to *The Miracle Morning for Couples 30-Day Transformation Challenge* and read ahead. This will give you the mindset and strategy to not only overcome any resistance you may have to starting, but it will give you the most effective process for implementing a new habit and sticking with it. Think of it as beginning with the end in mind.

From this day forward, starting with the next thirty days, keep your alarm set for thirty to sixty minutes earlier than you typically wake up so that you can start waking up when you *want* to, instead of when you *must*. It's time to start launching each day with a Miracle Morning so that you can become the person you need to be to take yourself, your partner, and your family to extraordinary levels.

What will you do with that extra time? You're going to find out in the next chapter, but for now, simply continue reading this book during your Miracle Morning until you learn the whole routine.

Step Two: Join The Miracle Morning Community at www.MyT-MMCommunity.com to connect with and get support from more than 180,000 like-minded early risers, many of whom have been generating extraordinary results with The Miracle Morning for years.

Step Three: Enroll your partner to join you on this adventure so you can encourage, support, and hold each other accountable to follow through until your Miracle Morning for Couples has become a lifelong habit.

Okay, now let's get into the six most powerful, proven personal development practices to propel your You Element to the highest degree known to man (or woman). Bringing these practices into your life has the potential to create the most legendary relationship you desire.

We introduce to you …The Life S.A.V.E.R.S.

— 3 —
YOU AND THE LIFE S.A.V.E.R.S.

Six Practices Guaranteed to Save You from a Life of Unfulfilled Potential

"What Hal has done with his acronym S.A.V.E.R.S. is take the best practices—developed over centuries of human consciousness development—and condensed the 'best of the best' into a daily morning ritual. A ritual that is now part of my day."

—ROBERT KIYOSAKI,
bestselling author of *Rich Dad Poor Dad*

*"It takes courage to grow up and become
who you really are."*

—E. E. CUMMINGS,
American poet, painter, essayist, author, and playwright

If you want to fix your relationship, you need to fix You. If you want to grow your relationship, you need to grow You. If you want to design the most amazing relationship possible, you need to design the most amazing You possible.

The challenge is that most people live their lives on the wrong side of a significant gap that separates who we are from who we can become, which holds us back from creating the life and relationship we truly want. Often frustrated with ourselves and our lack of consistent motivation, effort, and results in one or more areas of our lives, we spend too much time *thinking* about the actions we should be taking to create the results that we want and too little (or no) time actually taking those actions. More often than not, we *know* what we need to do; we just don't consistently *do* what we know.

It all begins with You. That's how it began for us. We both had our own journeys, different areas to develop. But the journey to creating the marriage we desired first had to start with ourselves.

Intimate relationships are one of the greatest vehicles for human growth and development. This is because as couples take the journey to enduring commitment, they must recognize the evolution and change of that relationship over time, continually adjusting targets, goals, and habits as they grow out of their old programming. Change and evolution *will* happen, whether you like it or not. You *will* be presented with challenges. You *will* have disagreements. *Truly coming to terms with this, and becoming proactive about it, will go a long way to continuing your own growth as a person, which in turn will go a long way in helping you and your partner build a long-standing, happy, and thriving relationship.*

The **You** is the "self" of your relationship. Before you and your spouse joined together, you were an independent being. You still are. Often, we begin to lose ourselves with the busyness of life and kids, but your relationship needs a strong You to thrive.

The You is your personal growth, self-awareness, confidence, health, and happiness. The You is your foundation of the relationship. Without working on your You, you can't bring your best self (or at least your "learning, growing, getting better" self) to the marriage and confidently engage the elements of PARTNERS, FRIENDS, and LOVERS.

Growing You is the single most important thing you can do to create a legendary relationship. A relationship of which you can be proud. A relationship from which you derive abundant joy. A relationship that will teach your children how to cultivate meaningful relationships of their own one day. Your kids learn from you how to treat themselves and how they should expect to be treated by others.

Standing on your own two feet is one of the essential building blocks in creating an intimate and enduring relationship. It establishes the boundaries that will permit emotional intimacy, even merging, between you and your partner, without fear of losing yourself.

This process is the foundation of the "You" that leads to the deeply connected "we."

While we have reached a pinnacle in connecting with new and old friends through social media, we have also become disconnected as a society more than ever. Yet relationships are our greatest asset. You are here to reverse the disconnection by being the best possible You, which translates into the best spouse/partner, which converts into being an amazing father/mother, and which then inspires your children to do the same. When you become the best You for yourself, your partner, and your kids, you leave a legacy for generations to come. *The Miracle Morning for Couples* is fundamentally grounded in the idea that a thriving and flourishing relationship requires that **two people must bring their best selves to the table before they can begin to create the deepest connection they desire.**

This is what the Life S.A.V.E.R.S. are designed for. When your own personal growth leads the way, the path to the most fulfilling relationship you can think of can be revealed.

But do you feel like the life and relationship that you want—and the person you know you need to be to create both—are just beyond your grasp? When you see other couples who are excelling in an area or playing at a level that you're not, does it ever seem like they've got it all figured out? Like they must know something that you don't know, because if you knew it you'd be excelling too? This is because each of them has built their individual You to a place that allows them to bring their best strengths to the marriage, to have the emotional intelligence, self-awareness, and mindset that grants them the best opportunity to create the relationship they desire with their significant other.

When Hal experienced the second of his two rock bottoms (the first was when he died for six minutes in a car crash, and the second was when his business failed due to the financial collapse of 2008), he felt lost and depressed. Applying what he already knew wasn't working. Nothing he tried was improving his situation. So, he began his own quest for the fastest, most effective strategy to take his success to the next level. He went in search of the best personal development practices that were being practiced by the world's most successful people.

After discovering and assembling a list of six of the most timeless, effective, and proven personal development practices, he first attempted to determine which one or two would accelerate his success the fastest. However, his breakthrough occurred when he asked himself, *what would happen if I did ALL of these?*

So, he did. Within just two months of implementing all six practices nearly every single day, Hal experienced what you might call "miraculous" results. He was able to more than double his income, and he went from someone who had never run more than a mile to training to run a 52-mile ultramarathon—ironic because he *wasn't* a runner and actually despised running. He thought, *what better way to take my physical, mental, emotional, and spiritual capacities to another level?*

When Brandy told Lance about the S.A.V.E.R.S., their marriage was at rock bottom. Lance began the practice of fixing himself, rebuilding his You Element, and becoming the man he wanted to be. These practices were his first step in saving his marriage with Brandy. They would forever change the trajectory of their relationship. They can do the same for you.

Whether you're already very successful, like multi-millionaire entrepreneur Robert Kiyosaki who practices The Miracle Morning and the S.A.V.E.R.S. almost every day, or you feel the person you know you can be is just beyond your grasp, the Life S.A.V.E.R.S. are virtually guaranteed to save you from missing out on the extraordinary life and relationship you truly want.

Why the S.A.V.E.R.S. Work

The S.A.V.E.R.S. are simple but profoundly effective daily morning practices that are virtually guaranteed to enable you to become more so that you can fulfill your potential. They also give you space to gain heightened levels of clarity, to plan and live your life on your terms. They're designed to start your day by putting you in a peak physical, mental, emotional, and spiritual state so that you continually improve, feel great and always perform at your best level.

We know, we know. You don't have time. Before starting The Miracle Morning, we would wake up to pure chaos, with barely enough time to get ourselves and our kids dressed, fed, and out the door for work and school. You probably think you can hardly squeeze in what you have to do already, never mind what you want to do. But we "didn't have time" before The Miracle Morning either. And yet, here we are with more time, more prosperity, and a more peaceful life than we've ever had before.

What you need to realize right now is that your Miracle Morning for Couples will create time for you. The Life S.A.V.E.R.S. are the vehicle to help you reconnect with your true essence and wake up with purpose instead of obligation. The practices help you build energy, see priorities more clearly, and find the most productive flow in your life.

In other words, the Life S.A.V.E.R.S. don't take time from your day but ultimately add more to it.

Each letter in S.A.V.E.R.S. represents one of the best practices of the most successful people on the planet. From A-list movie stars and world-class professional athletes to CEOs and entrepreneurs, you'd be hard-pressed to find an elite performer who didn't swear by at least one of the S.A.V.E.R.S.

That's what makes The Miracle Morning so effective; you're harnessing the game-changing benefits of not just one but all six of *the best practices, developed over centuries of human consciousness development* and combining them all into a concise, fully customizable morning ritual.

The S.A.V.E.R.S. are:

Silence

Affirmations

Visualization

Exercise

Reading

Scribing

Leveraging these six practices is how you will accelerate your personal development by maximizing the impact of your newfound Miracle Morning ritual. They're customizable to fit you, your lifestyle, your business, and your specific goals. And you can start implementing them first thing tomorrow morning.

Let's go through each of the S.A.V.E.R.S. in detail.

S is for Silence

Silence, the first practice of the Life S.A.V.E.R.S., is a key habit for beginning the journey of improving your You Element so that you can bring your best self to the relationship. If you've been guilty of starting your day by immediately grabbing your phone or computer and diving into emails, phone calls, social media, and text messages, then this is your opportunity to learn the power of beginning each day with peaceful, purposeful *silence*.

Like we did before The Miracle Morning, most people start the day when their alarm signifies they *must* get up. And most people run from morning to night, struggling to regain control for the rest of the day. It's not a coincidence. Starting each day with a period of silence instead will immediately reduce your stress levels and help you begin the day with the kind of calm and clarity that you need to focus on what's most important.

Remember, many of the world's most successful people are daily practitioners of silence. That shows you how important it is. It's not surprising that Oprah practices stillness—or that she does nearly all of the other Life S.A.V.E.R.S. too. Musician Katy Perry practices transcendental meditation, as do Sheryl Crow and Sir Paul McCartney. Film and television stars Jennifer Aniston, Ellen DeGeneres, Jerry Seinfeld, Howard Stern, Cameron Diaz, Clint Eastwood, and Hugh Jackman have all spoken of their daily meditation practice. Hip-hop mogul Russell Simmons meditates with his two daughters every morning for 20 minutes. Even famous billionaires Ray Dalio and Rupert Murdoch have attributed their financial success to the daily practice of stillness. You'll be in good (and quiet) company by doing the same.

If it seems like we're asking you to do nothing, let's clarify: you have many choices for your practice of silence. In no particular order, here are a few to get you started:

- Meditation

- Prayer

- Reflection

- Deep breathing

- Gratitude

Whichever you choose, be sure you don't stay in bed for your period of silence, and better still, get out of your bedroom altogether.

In an interview with *Shape* magazine, actress and singer Kristen Bell said, "Do meditative yoga for 10 minutes every morning. When you have a problem—whether it's road rage, your guy, or work—meditation allows everything to unfold the way it's supposed to."

And don't be afraid to expand your horizons. Meditation comes in many forms. As Angelina Jolie told *Stylist* magazine, "I find meditation in sitting on the floor with the kids coloring for an hour or going on the trampoline. You do what you love, that makes you happy, and that gives you your meditation."

The Benefits of Silence

How many times do we find ourselves in stressful situations? How many times do we deal with immediate needs that take us away from our vision or plan? How often do our spouse and kids trigger us? Stress is one of the most common side effects of being in a sucky, disconnected relationship. We face the ever-present distractions of other people encroaching on our schedule and the inevitable fires we must extinguish. Our spouses and our children have the uncanny ability to push our stress buttons. After a long day of work, we often feel we have little to give to our relationship. The need to decompress can override our desire to connect with our partner, leading to a slippery slope of being detached and disengaged from our family. This can even lead to opportunities for arguments and frustration.

Excessive stress is terrible for your health. It triggers your fight-or-flight response, and that releases a cascade of toxic hormones that can stay in your body for days. Which is fine, if you experience that type of stress only occasionally.

According to PsychologyToday.com, "The stress hormone, cortisol, is public health enemy number one. Scientists have known for years that elevated cortisol levels: interfere with learning and memory, lower immune function and bone density, increase weight gain, blood pressure, cholesterol, heart disease—the list goes on and on. Chronic stress and elevated cortisol levels also increase the risk for depression, mental illness, and lower life expectancy."

Silence in the form of meditation reduces stress and, as a result, improves your health. A major study run by several groups—including the National Institutes of Health, the American Medical Association, the Mayo Clinic, and scientists from both Harvard and Stanford—revealed that meditation reduces stress and high blood pressure. A recent study by Dr. Norman Rosenthal, a world-renowned psychiatrist who works with the David Lynch Foundation, even found that people who practice meditation are 30 percent less likely to die from heart disease.

Another study from Harvard found that just eight weeks of meditation could lead to "increased gray-matter density in the hippocampus, known to be important for learning and memory, and in structures associated with self-awareness, compassion, and introspection."

Meditation helps you slow down and focus on you, even if it's for just a short time. Starting your meditation practice can help you say goodbye to the "mommy brain" that plagues many busy, overwhelmed moms (and dads!).

"I started meditating because I felt like I needed to stop my life from running me," singer Sheryl Crow has said. "So meditation for me helped slow my day down." She continues to devote 20 minutes in the morning and 20 minutes at night to meditation.

Dan Harris, correspondent for ABC News, anchor of *Nightline*, co-anchor of *Good Morning America*, and author of *10% Happier: How I Tamed the Voice in My Head, Reduced Stress Without Losing My Edge, and Found Self-Help That Actually Works--A True Story*, has one of the best stories for how meditation positively impacted his life. Harris had an on-air panic attack in June of 2004 in front of five million watchers (you can easily find it on YouTube). He was gasping for air, lost his ability to speak, and had to bail out of his report on live television! Harris claims that this panic attack was induced by the anxiety from the stress of his job as a journalist (among other things) and prompted him to seek help to alleviate it. That search led him to meditation, which allows Dan to "act wisely instead of react blindly" to the situations and challenges that we all face in our lives. These can include telling ourselves we aren't good enough, letting all of the thoughts in our mind control us or make us less aware, or being triggered and angered by the things our spouses and children do that frustrate and bring us stress. He can now attest, as he does through his books and podcast, that this practice has changed his life in ways he couldn't have imagined.

Being silent opens a space for you to secure your own oxygen mask before assisting others. The benefits are extraordinary and can bring you much-needed clarity and peace of mind. Practicing silence, in other words, can help you reduce your stress, improve cognitive performance, and become confident at the same time.

Guided Meditations and Meditation Apps

Meditation is like anything else—if you've never done it before, then it can be difficult or feel awkward at first. If you are a first-time meditator, we recommend starting with a guided meditation.

Since meditation has become popular in the last ten years, there are many resources and tools to get you started. There is something for everyone! Here are a few of our favorite meditation apps that are available for both iPhone/iPad and Android devices:

- Headspace

- Calm

- Omvana

- Simply Being

- Insight Timer

There are subtle and significant differences among these meditation apps, one of which is the voice of the person speaking.

If you don't have a device that allows you to download apps, simply go to YouTube or Google and search for the keywords "guided meditation." You can also search by duration (e.g. "five-minute guided meditation") or topic (e.g. "guided meditation for increased confidence").

Miracle Morning (Individual) Meditation

When you're ready to try meditating on your own, here is a simple, step-by-step meditation you can use during your Miracle Morning, even if you've never done this before.

- Before beginning, it's important to prepare yourself and set expectations. This is a time for you to quiet your mind and let go of the compulsive need to constantly be thinking about something—reliving the past or worrying about the future but never living fully in the present. This is the time to let go of your stresses, take a break from worrying about your problems, and be here in this moment. It is a time to access the essence of who you truly are—to go deeper than what you have, what you do or the labels you've accepted. If this sounds foreign, or too much like New Age, that's okay. I've felt the same way. It's probably because you've never tried it before. But thankfully, you're about to.

- Find a quiet, comfortable place to sit. You can sit on the couch, a chair, the floor, or a pillow for added comfort.

- Sit upright, cross-legged. You can close your eyes, or you can look down at a point on the ground about two feet in front of you.

- Begin by focusing on your breath while taking slow, deep breaths. Breathe in through the nose and out through the mouth. The most effective breathing causes your belly, rather than your chest, to expand.

- Now, start pacing your breath: breathe in slowly for a count of three seconds (one one-thousand, two one-thousand, three one-thousand), hold it in for another three counts, and then breathe out slowly for a final count of three. Feel your thoughts and emotions settling down as you focus on your breath. Be aware that, as you attempt to quiet your mind, thoughts will still come in to pay a visit. Simply acknowledge them and then let them go, always returning your focus to your breath.

- Allow yourself to be fully present in this moment. This is often referred to as "being." Not thinking, not doing, just being. Continue to follow your breath, and imagine inhaling positive, loving, and peaceful energy and exhaling all your worries and stress. Enjoy the quiet. Enjoy the moment. Just breathe … Just be.

- If you find that you have a constant influx of thoughts, it may be helpful for you to focus on a single word, phrase, or mantra and repeat it over and over again to yourself as you inhale and exhale. For example, you might try something like this: (On the inhale) "I inhale confidence … " (As you exhale) "I exhale fear … " You can swap the word "confidence" for whatever you feel you need to bring more of into your life (love, faith, energy, etc.), and swap the word "fear" with whatever you feel you need to let go of (stress, worry, resentment, etc.). You can even focus just on your breath, counting "one" on the inhale and "two" on the exhale. After each ten count, begin again at one.

Meditation is a gift you can give yourself every day. Our time spent meditating has become one of our favorite parts of The Miracle Morning routine. It's a time to be at peace and to experience gratitude and freedom from our day-to-day stressors and worries.

Think of daily meditation as a temporary vacation from your problems. Although your problems will still be there when you finish your daily meditation, you'll find that you're more centered and better equipped to solve them.

A is for Affirmations

Have you ever wondered how some people seem to just be good at *everything* they do and consistently achieve at a level so high, you can hardly comprehend how you're ever going to join them? Or why others seem to drop every ball? Time and time again, it is a person's *mindset* that has proven to be the driving factor in their results.

Mindset can be defined as the accumulation of a person's beliefs, attitudes, and emotional intelligence. In her bestselling book, *Mindset: The New Psychology of Success*, Carol Dweck, Ph.D., states: "For twenty years, my research has shown that the view you adopt of yourself profoundly affects the way you lead your life."

Others can easily sense your mindset. It shows up undeniably in your language, your confidence, and your demeanor. Your mindset affects everything! Show us a couple with a successful mindset, and we'll show you a successful relationship.

We know firsthand, though, how difficult it can be to maintain the right mindset—the confidence and enthusiasm, not to mention motivation—during the roller coaster ride that comes with being an intimate couple. Mindset is largely something we adopt without conscious thought; at a subconscious level, we have been programmed to think, believe, act, and talk to ourselves a certain way.

Our programming comes from many influences, including what others have told us, what we tell ourselves, and all of our good and bad life experiences. That programming expresses itself in every area of our lives, including the way we behave around our children. And that means, if we want a better family dynamic, we need better mental programming.

Affirmations are a tool for doing just that. They enable you to become more intentional about your goals while also providing the encouragement and positive mindset necessary to achieve them. When you repeatedly tell yourself who you want to be, what you want to accomplish, and how you are going to achieve it, your subconscious mind will shift your beliefs and behavior. Once you believe and act in new ways, you will begin to manifest your affirmations into reality.

Science has proven that affirmations—when done correctly—are one of the most effective tools for quickly becoming the person you need to be to achieve everything you want in your life—for yourself and your family. And yet, affirmations also get a bad rap. Many people have tried them only to be disappointed, with little or no results. However, there is a way to leverage affirmations in a way that will absolutely produce results for you in your relationship

By repeatedly articulating and reinforcing to yourself **what** result you want to accomplish, **why** accomplishing it is important to you, **which** specific actions are required to produce that result, and, most importantly, precisely **when** you will commit to taking those actions, your subconscious mind will shift your beliefs and behavior. You'll begin to automatically believe and act in new ways and eventually manifest your affirmations into your reality. But first…

Why the Old Way of Doing Affirmations Does Not Work

For decades, countless so-called experts and gurus have taught affirmations in ways that have proven to be ineffective and set people up for failure. Following are two of the most common problems with affirmations.

Problem #1: Lying to Yourself Doesn't Work

I am a millionaire. Really?

I am the most amazing husband/wife I can truly be. Are you?

I have 7 percent body fat. Do you?

I have achieved all of my goals this year. Have you?

Creating affirmations as if you've already become or achieved something may be the single biggest cause of affirmations not being effective.

With this technique, every time you recite the affirmation that isn't rooted in truth, your subconscious will resist it. As an intelligent human being who isn't delusional, lying to yourself repeatedly will never be the optimum strategy. *The truth will always prevail.*

Problem #2: Passive Language Doesn't Produce Results

Many affirmations have been designed to make you feel good by creating an empty promise of something you desire. For example, here is a popular money affirmation that's been perpetuated by many world-famous gurus:

I am a money magnet. Money flows to me effortlessly and in abundance.

This type of affirmation might make you feel good in the moment by giving you a false sense of relief from your financial worries, but it won't generate any income. People who sit back and wait for money to show up magically are cash poor.

To generate the kind of abundance you want (or any result you desire, for that matter), you've got to actually do something. Your actions must be aligned with your desired results, and your affirmations must articulate and affirm both.

Four Steps to Create Affirmations that Improve Your Relationship

Here are simple steps to create and implement results-oriented Miracle Morning affirmations that will program your conscious and subconscious mind, while redirecting your conscious mind to upgrade your behavior so that you can begin to produce results and take your levels of personal and professional success beyond what you've ever experienced before.

Step One: Determine the Legendary Result You Are Committed to and Why

Notice I'm not starting with what you *want*. Everyone wants things, but we don't get what we want: we get what we're committed to. You want to be a great role model for your kids? Who doesn't? Join that non-exclusive club. Oh, wait, you're 100 percent committed to becoming the best husband or wife possible by clarifying and executing the necessary actions until the result is achieved? Okay, now we're talking.

Action: Start by writing down a specific, extraordinary result or outcome—one that challenges you, which would significantly improve your life, and that you are ready to commit to creating—even if you're not yet sure how you will do it. Then reinforce your commitment by including your *why*, the compelling reason you're willing to stay committed.

Examples: *I am dedicated to going on a date night once a week with my significant other to model a healthy love relationship for my children.*

Or ...

I am 100 percent committed to being as healthy as I can be so that I have the energy to be fully present with my children and spouse.

Or …

I will meditate 10 minutes a day to help me practice letting go of the things that trigger me so that I show less anger toward my spouse and children.

Step Two: Decide the Necessary Actions You Are Committed to Taking and *When*

Writing an affirmation that merely affirms what you *want* without affirming what you are committed to *doing* is one step above pointless and can be counterproductive. It is tricking your subconscious mind into thinking that the result will happen automatically, without effort.

Action: Clarify the (specific) action, activity, or habit that is required for you to achieve your ideal outcome, and clearly state when and how often you will execute the necessary action.

Examples: *To ensure I have a date night weekly with my significant other, I am 100 percent committed to lining up a babysitter, choosing an activity, and blocking time in my calendar by Wednesday of each week for the upcoming weekend.*

Or …

To ensure that I am as healthy as I can be, I am 100 percent committed to going to the gym five days per week and running on the treadmill for a minimum of 20 minutes each day from 6:00 a.m. to 7:00 a.m.

Or …

So that I can diminish the amount of anger toward the things that trigger me, I will meditate for 10 minutes every morning as part of my Life S.A.V.E.R.S. routine.

The more *specific* your affirmations are, the better. Be sure to include *frequency* (how often), *quantity* (how many), and *precise time frames* (when you will begin and end your activities).

Step Three: Recite Your Affirmations Every Morning (with Emotion)

Remember, your Miracle Morning affirmations aren't designed merely to make you *feel good.* These written statements are strategically engineered to program your subconscious mind with the beliefs and mindset you need to achieve your desired outcomes in your relationship. All of this while directing your conscious mind to keep you focused on your highest priorities and the actions that will get you there.

For your affirmations to be effective, however, it is important that you tap into your emotions while reciting them. Mindlessly repeating an affirmation without intentionally feeling its truth will have minimal impact for you. You must take responsibility for generating authentic emotions, such as excitement and determination, and powerfully infusing those emotions in every affirmation you recite.

You must affirm who you need to be to do the things you need to do so that you can have the results that you want. We'll say this again: it isn't magic. This strategy works when you connect with *the person you need to become* on the way to achieving your goals. It's who you are that attracts your results, more than any other activity.

Action: Schedule time each day to read your affirmations during your Miracle Morning to both program your subconscious and focus your conscious mind on what's most important to you and what you are committed to doing to make it your reality. That's right, you must read them daily. Reading your affirmations occasionally is as effective as an occasional workout. You'll start seeing results only when you've made them a part of your daily routine.

You can remind yourself to recite your affirmations often by putting them anywhere you can: under your car's sun visor, taped to your mirror. A great place to read affirmations is in the shower. If you laminate them and leave them there, then they will be in front of you every day. You can even write them directly on a mirror with dry erase markers. The more you see them, the more the subconscious mind can connect with them to change your thinking and your actions.

Step Four: Constantly Update and Evolve Your Affirmations

As you continue to grow, improve, and evolve, so should your affirmations. When you come up with a new goal, dream, or extraordinary result you want to create for your life and relationship, add it to your affirmations.

Personally, we have affirmations for every significant area of our lives (marriage, finances, health, happiness, friendships, parenting, etc.), and we continually update them as we learn more. We are always on the lookout for quotes (as you'll see, this book is littered with them!), strategies, and philosophies that we can add to improve our mindset. Any time you come across an empowering quote or philosophy and think to yourself, *Wow, that is an area where I could make a huge improvement*, add it to your affirmations.

Remember, your affirmations should be tailored to you and how you want to show up in your life and relationship, along with being phrased in the form of "I" statements. They must be specific for them to work in your subconscious.

Your programming can change and improve at any time, starting right now. You can reprogram any perceived limitations with new beliefs and create new behaviors, so you can become as successful as you want to be in any area of life you choose.

In summary, your new affirmations articulate the extraordinary results you are committed to creating, why they are critically important to you, and, most importantly, which necessary actions you are committed to taking and when to ensure that you attain and sustain the extraordinary levels of success you truly want (and deserve) for your life.

Affirmations to Create a Legendary Relationship

In addition to the formula to create your affirmations, we have included this list of sample affirmations, which may help spark your creativity. Here's a bonus tip: after you've created your relationship affirmations, share them with your partner. Consider working together to create affirmations that help cast the vision the two of you have with each other.

- I am just as worthy, deserving, and capable of achieving a legendary relationship as any other person on earth, and I will prove that today with my actions.

- I desire my relationship with my spouse to serve as a model for what I want my children to have in the future, and I will begin this by becoming a better listener.

- Where I am now is a result of who I *was*, but where I go and how I grow depends entirely on who I *choose to be*, starting today.

- The change in my relationship begins with *me*. I am fully committed to dedicating 30-60 minutes each day to do my Miracle Morning and the S.A.V.E.R.S. so that I can continue to become the person I need to be to create the relationship I want for my life.

- I focus on learning new things and improving my You Element daily, and I commit to reading or re-reading at least one book to help that effort every month.

- I am fully committed to empowering and inspiring my partner by sharing the knowledge I learn that is helping me grow
  each and every day.

- I am committed to constant and never-ending improvement
  in the tasks necessary for my optimal day-to-day functioning.

- I will choose to love my partner exactly as he/she is today and
  will create a list of reasons I love him/her and read it to myself
  every day, committing it to memory.

- I commit to an unplugged family meal five nights a week so
  that we can strengthen our family as a group and stay connected to each other.

These are just a few examples of affirmations. You can use any
that resonate with you but do also create your own using the four-
step formula described in the previous pages. Remember, anything
you repeatedly say to yourself with emotion will be programmed into
your subconscious mind, help you form new beliefs, and manifest
through your actions. Lastly, be sure to share your affirmations with
your partner!

V is for Visualization

Visualization has long been a well-known practice of world-class
athletes, who use it to optimize their performance. Olympic athletes
and top performers in many categories incorporate visualization as
a critical part of their daily training. What is less well known is that
those who are in happy, successful relationships use it just as frequently.

Visualization is a technique in which you use your imagination
to create a compelling picture of your future, providing you with

heightened clarity and producing the motivation that will assist you in making your vision a reality.

If you'd like some fascinating information about *why* visualization works, just Google "mirror neurons." A neuron is a cell that connects the brain and other parts of the body; a mirror neuron fires when we take action or observe someone else taking action. This is a relatively new area of study in neurology, but these cells seem to allow us to improve our abilities by watching other people perform activities *or* by visualizing ourselves performing them. Some studies indicate that experienced weightlifters can increase muscle mass through vivid visualization sessions, and mirror neurons get the credit for making this possible. In many ways, the brain can't tell the difference between a vivid visualization and an actual experience. Crazy, right?

What Do You Visualize?

Most couples are limited by visions of their past results, replaying previous failures and heartbreaks. Additionally, this leads to repeated patterns of inefficient conflict resolution that only serves to fix a challenge short-term. Creative visualization, on the other hand, enables you to design the vision that will occupy your mind, ensuring that the greatest pull on you is your future—a compelling, exciting, and limitless future. It helps couples get beyond the starting line of repair to catapult them to the relationship they truly desire.

So, how do you visualize? After reading your affirmations, sit upright, close your eyes, and take a few slow, deep breaths. For the next five to ten minutes, simply visualize the *specific actions* that are necessary for your long- and short-term goals to become a reality.

Notice that we did *not* say to visualize the results. Many people will disagree on this, but there are studies that provide scientific evidence showing that merely visualizing the result you want (e.g., the new car, the dream house, crossing the finish line, standing on stage, etc.) can diminish your drive because your brain has already experienced the reward on some level. Instead, we highly recommend focusing your visualization on the necessary actions, more so than just the results. Visualize yourself taking the actions—especially the actions that you habitually resist and procrastinate on—in a way that creates a compelling mental and emotional experience of the action. For example, Hal despised running, but he had made a commitment to himself (and publicly) to run a 52-mile ultra-marathon. Throughout the course of his five months of training, he used Miracle Morning visualizations to see himself lacing up his running shoes and hitting the pavement—*with a smile on his face and pep in his step*—so that when it was time to train, he had already programmed the experience to be positive and enjoyable.

You might picture yourself having fun and light conversations with your partner. Spend time imagining talking with each other at dinner, for example. What does it look like? How does it feel as you develop a great relationship? Picture yourself responding to obstacles and issues.

You can pick anything that is a critical action step or skill that you may not be performing at your best yet. Envisioning success and what it takes to get there will prepare you for, and almost ensure, a successful day with your partner.

Three Simple Steps for Miracle Morning Visualization

The perfect time to visualize yourself living in alignment with your affirmations is right after you read them.

Step One: Get Ready

Some people like to play instrumental music, such as classical or baroque, in the background during their visualization. Just make sure it's something without lyrics that can distract you. Lance listens to an excellent playlist on Spotify called "Music for Concentration." If you'd like to experiment with music, put it on with the volume relatively low.

Now, sit up tall in a comfortable position. This can be on a chair, the couch, or the floor with a cushion. Breathe deeply. Close your eyes, clear your mind, and let go of any self-imposed limitations as you prepare yourself for the benefits of visualization.

Step Two: Visualize What You Really Want

Many people don't feel comfortable visualizing success and are even scared to succeed. Some people may experience resistance in this area. Some may even feel guilty that they will leave the other 95 percent behind when they become successful.

This famous quote from Marianne Williamson is a great reminder for anyone who feels mental or emotional obstacles when attempting to visualize: "Our deepest fear is not that we are inadequate. Our deepest fear is that we are powerful beyond measure. It is our light, not our darkness that most frightens us. We ask ourselves, 'Who am I to be brilliant, gorgeous, talented, fabulous?' Actually, who are you not to be? You are a child of God. Your playing small does not serve the world. There is nothing enlightened about shrinking so that other people won't feel insecure around you. We are all meant to shine, as children do. We were born to make manifest the glory of God that is within us. It's not just in some of us; itis in everyone and as we let our own light shine, we unconsciously give other people permission to do the same. As we are liberated from our own fear, our presence automatically liberates others."

Consider that the greatest gift you can give to those you love is to live to your full potential. What does that look like for you? What do you really want? Forget about logic, limits, and being practical.

If you could reach any heights, personally and professionally, what would that look like?

See, feel, hear, touch, taste, and smell every detail of your vision. Involve all your senses to maximize effectiveness. The more vivid you make your vision, the more compelled you'll be to take the necessary actions to make it a reality.

Step Three: Visualize Yourself Taking (and Enjoying) the Necessary Actions

Once you've created a clear mental picture of what you want, begin to see yourself doing precisely what you need to do to achieve your vision, moving with supreme confidence and enjoying every step of the process. See yourself engaged in the actions you'll need to take (exercising, writing, selling, presenting, public speaking, making calls, sending emails, etc.). Picture yourself with a look and *feeling* of supreme confidence as you sit with your partner, engaged in meaningful conversation. Imagine yourself present, listening, and focused. See and *feel* yourself smiling as you're running on that treadmill, filled with a sense of pride for your self-discipline to follow through. In other words, visualize yourself doing what you must do, and thoroughly enjoying the process, especially if it's a process you don't naturally enjoy. Imagine what it would look and feel like if you did enjoy it.

Picture the look of determination on your face as you confidently and consistently connect with your partner, listen to their needs, and take action based on what you observe. See yourself as the spouse who is calm, confident, and prepared. Imagine the ease you have around each other. Picture yourself planning date nights, making the arrangements. Imagine you and your partner trying that new activity you've always wanted to do. Visualize the smile and laughter from your family as they respond to a happier You.

Seeing yourself as the person who has it all together is the first step in actually *getting* it all together.

Final Thoughts on Visualization

When you combine reading your affirmations every morning with daily visualization, you will turbocharge the programming of your subconscious mind for success through peak performance. When you visualize daily, you align your thoughts, feelings, and behaviors with your vision, making it easier to maintain the motivation you need to continue taking the necessary actions. It helps to build your confidence, show up, and nurture and amplify the You Element, bringing your best self to your relationship. Visualization can be a powerful aid in overcoming self-limiting beliefs, as well as self-limiting habits, such as procrastination, and get you into the actions necessary to achieve extraordinary results.

E is for Exercise

Exercise should be a staple of your Miracle Morning. Even a few minutes of exercise each day significantly enhances your health, improves your self-confidence and emotional well-being, and enables you to think better and concentrate longer. You'll also notice how quickly your energy increases with daily exercise, and your partner will notice it too.

Personal development experts and self-made multi-millionaire entrepreneurs Eben Pagan and Tony Robbins (who is also a best-selling author) both agree that the number-one key to success is to start every morning with a personal success ritual. Included in both of their success rituals is some type of morning exercise. Eben articulates the importance of *morning* exercise: "Every morning, you've got to get your heart rate up and get your blood flowing and fill your lungs with oxygen." He continued, "Don't just exercise at the end of the day, or at the middle of the day. And even if you do like to exercise at those times, always incorporate at least 10 to 20 minutes of jumping jacks or some sort of aerobic exercise in the morning." Hey, if it works for Eben and Tony, it will work for me (and you)!

Lest you think you must engage in triathlon or marathon training, think again. Your morning exercise also doesn't need to replace an afternoon or evening regimen if you already have one in place. You can still hit the gym at the usual time. However, the benefits from adding as little as five minutes of morning exercise are undeniable, including improved blood pressure and blood sugar levels and decreased risk of all kinds of scary things, like heart disease, osteoporosis, cancer, and diabetes. Maybe most importantly, a little exercise in the morning will increase your energy levels for the rest of the day to help you keep up with your demanding schedule.

You can go for a walk or run, follow along to a yoga video on YouTube, or do a few sets of squats, pushups, and sit-ups. There's also an excellent app called 7 Minute Workout that gives you a full-body workout in—you guessed it—seven minutes. The choice is yours, but pick one activity and do it.

Being the best for your relationship isn't easy. It takes dedication and focus. You need an endless reserve of energy to make the best of the challenges that come your way, and a daily morning exercise practice is going to provide it.

Exercise for Your Brain

Even if you don't care about your physical health, consider that exercise is simply going to make you smarter, and that can only help your problem-solving abilities. Dr. Steven Masley, a Florida physician and nutritionist with a health practice geared toward executives, explains how exercise creates a direct connection to your cognitive ability.

"If we're talking about brain performance, the best predictor of brain speed is aerobic capacity—how well you can run up a hill is very strongly correlated with brain speed and cognitive shifting ability," Masley said.

Masley has designed a corporate wellness program based on the work he's done with more than 1,000 patients. "The average person going into these programs will increase brain speed by 25-30 percent."

Lance does bodyweight exercises in the morning. He does a pyramid workout (reps of 5-10-15-10-5) of various exercises that takes only 10-15 minutes. Brandy walks up and down the hill of our street listening to an inspirational podcast (exercise for her brain, too!). Hal chose yoga for his exercise activity and began practicing it shortly after he created The Miracle Morning. He's loved it ever since.

Final Thoughts on Exercise

You know that if you want to maintain good health and increase your energy, you must exercise consistently. That's not news to anyone. But what also isn't news is how easy it is to make excuses. Two of the biggest are "I don't have time" and "I'm too tired." Those are just the first two on the list; there is no limit to the excuses you can produce. And the more creative you are, the more excuses you can find!

The beauty of incorporating exercise into your Miracle Morning is that it happens before your day wears you out and before you have an entire day to come up with new excuses. Because it comes first, The Miracle Morning is a surefire way to avoid those excuses and make exercise a daily habit.

Legal disclaimer: hopefully this goes without saying, but you should consult your doctor or physician before beginning any exercise regimen, especially if you are experiencing any physical pain, discomfort, disabilities, etc. You may need to modify or even refrain from an exercise routine to meet your individual needs.

R is for Reading

One of the fastest ways to achieve everything you want is to find successful people to be your role models. For every goal you have, there's a good chance an expert out there has already achieved the same thing or something similar. As Tony Robbins says, "Success leaves clues."

Fortunately, some of the best of the best have shared their stories in writing. And that means all those success blueprints are just waiting to be discovered by anyone willing to invest the time in reading. Books are a limitless supply of help and mentorship right at your fingertips.

If you are already a reader, great! But if up until this point you've been a part of the majority of our society content to clock in and out, putting forth minimal effort for moderate compensation, you have an incredible opportunity here.

Occasionally, we hear someone say, "I'm so busy, I don't have time to read." We get it. There are other ways to invest a little time with books. Listening to an audiobook (and journaling while doing it—BONUS!) is another way to "read." We also really like Brian Johnson's *Philosopher's Notes*, where he breaks down the big ideas of his favorite books, most of which are big sellers in the personal growth category.

You have one, ten, or even twenty minutes every day to take in valuable content to enrich your life. Just use some of the strategies shared earlier in this book, spend five fewer minutes on Facebook before you start your day, or read while eating lunch to nourish your mind and body simultaneously.

Here are some books we suggest you start with, and once you've primed your reading pump, we bet you'll keep going and never stop!

On Relationships and Love:

- *The Seven Principles for Making Marriage Work* by Dr. John Gottman

- *The Five Love Languages* by Gary Chapman

- *Love: What Life is All About...* by Leo Buscaglia

- *The Mastery of Love* by Don Miguel Ruiz

- *No More Mr. Nice Guy* by Robert Glover (for men)

- *Love is Letting Go of Fear* by Gerald Jampolsky

On Mindset:

- *Mindset: The New Psychology of Success* by Carol Dweck, PhD

- *The Art of Exceptional Living* by Jim Rohn

- *The One Thing: The Surprisingly Simple Truth Behind Extraordinary Results* by Gary Keller and Jay Papasan

- *The 7 Habits of Highly Effective People: Powerful Lessons in Personal Change* by Stephen R. Covey

- *Mastery* by Robert Greene

- *The 4 Hour Workweek: Escape 9-5, Live Anywhere, and Join the New Rich* by Tim Ferriss

- *The Game of Life and How to Play It* by Florence Scovel Shinn

- *The Compound Effect* by Darren Hardy

- *Taking Life Head On: How to Love the Life You Have While You Create the Life of Your Dreams* by Hal Elrod

- *Think and Grow Rich* by Napoleon Hill

- *Vision to Reality: How Short Term Massive Action Equals Long Term Maximum Results* and *Business Dating: Applying Relationship Rules in Business for Ultimate Success* by Honorée Corder

- *Finding Your Element: How to Discover Your Talents and Passions and Transform Your Life* by Sir Ken Robinson and Lou Aronica

- *Spirit Led Instead: The Little Tool Book of Limitless Transformation* by Jenai Lane

In addition to finding confidence in your relationship, you can increase your self-confidence, improve your communication skills, learn how to become healthy, and improve any other area of your life you can think of. Head to your library or local bookstore—or do what we do and visit Amazon.com—and you'll find more books than you can possibly imagine on any area of your life you want to improve.

For a complete list of Hal's favorite personal development books—including those that have made the biggest impact on his success and happiness—check out the Recommended Reading list at TMMBook.com.

How Much Should You Read?

We recommend making a commitment to read a minimum of ten pages per day (although five is okay to start with if you read slowly or don't yet enjoy reading).

Ten pages may not seem like a lot, but let's do the math. Reading ten pages per day adds up to 3,650 pages per year, which stacks up to approximately eighteen 200-page books that will enable you to take yourself to the next level so that you can take your relationship to the next level. All in just 10-15 minutes of daily reading, or 15-30 minutes if you read more slowly.

If you read eighteen personal and/or relationship development books in the next twelve months, do you think you'll improve your mindset, gain more confidence, and learn proven strategies that will accelerate your relationship success? Do you think you'll be a better, more capable version of who you are today? Do you think that will be reflected in your relationship results? Absolutely! Reading ten pages per day is not going to break you, but it will absolutely make you.

Final Thoughts on Reading

- Begin with the end in mind—what do you hope to gain from the book? Take a moment to do this now by asking yourself what you want to gain from reading *The Miracle Morning for Couples*.

- Books don't have to be read cover to cover, nor do they have to be finished. Remember that this is *your* reading time. Use the table of contents to make sure you are reading the parts you care about most and don't hesitate to put it down and move to another book if you aren't enjoying it. There is too much incredible information out there to spend any time on the mediocre.

- Many Miracle Morning practitioners use their reading time to catch up on their religious texts, such as the Bible or the Torah.

- Unless you're borrowing a book from the library or a friend, feel free to underline, circle, highlight, dog-ear, and take notes in the margins of the book. The process of marking books as you read allows you to come back at any time and recapture the key lessons, ideas, and benefits without needing to read the book again cover to cover. If you use a digital reader, such as Kindle, Nook, or iBooks, notes, and highlighting are easily organized so you can see them each time you flip through the book, or you can go directly to a list of your notes and highlights.

- Summarize key ideas, remarkable insights, and memorable passages in a journal. You can build your own summary of your favorite books so you can revisit the key content any time in just minutes.

- Rereading good personal development books is an underused yet very effective strategy. Rarely can you read a book once and internalize all its value. Achieving mastery in any area requires repetition. We've read *Mindset: The New Psychology of Success* by Carol Dweck as many as three times and often refer to it throughout the year. We even use its teachings with our daughters! Why not try it out with this book? Commit to rereading it as soon as you're finished to deepen your learning and give yourself more time to master your Miracle Morning.

- Audiobooks count as reading! You still get the information, and you can listen while exercising or during your commute. When I really want to study a book, I listen to the audio while looking at the text. This way I can take notes and underline text without slowing down too much. I am a pretty slow reader, but with audiobooks, I can listen at 1.5 or 2 times the speed and "read" much faster.

- Most importantly, quickly implement what you read. Schedule time to implement what you're reading, *while you're read-*

ing it. Literally read with your schedule next to you, and schedule time blocks to put the content into action. Share your learnings with your partner! Don't become a personal development junkie who reads a lot but does very little. We've met many people who take pride in the number of books they read, like some badge of honor. We'd rather read and implement one good book than to read ten books and then do nothing other than start reading the eleventh book. While reading is a great way to gain knowledge, insights, and strategies, it is the implementation and practice of these new strategies that will advance your life and relationship. Are you committed to implementing what you're learning in this book by taking action and following through with the 30-Day Challenge at the end?

Glad to hear it. Let's get to the final "S" of the S.A.V.E.R.S.

S is for Scribing

Scribing is simply another word for writing. Let's keep it real—Hal needed an "S" for the end of S.A.V.E.R.S. because a "W" wouldn't fit anywhere. Thanks, Thesaurus®; we owe you one.

The scribing element of your Miracle Morning enables you to write down what you're grateful for, as well as to document your insights, ideas, breakthroughs, realizations, successes, and lessons learned, as well as any areas of opportunity, personal growth, or improvement.

Most Miracle Morning practitioners scribe in a journal for five to ten minutes during their Miracle Morning. By getting your thoughts out of your head and putting them in writing, you'll immediately gain heightened awareness, clarity, and valuable insights to which you'd otherwise be oblivious.

If you're like Hal used to be, you probably have at least a few half-used and barely touched journals and notebooks. It wasn't until he started his own Miracle Morning practice that scribing quickly became one of his favorite daily habits. As Tony Robbins has said many times, "A life worth living is a life worth recording."

Writing will give you the daily benefits of consciously directing your thoughts, but what's even more powerful are the insights you'll gain from reviewing your journals, from cover to cover, afterward—especially at the end of the year.

It is hard to put into words how overwhelmingly constructive the experience of going back and reviewing your journals can be. Michael Maher, *The Miracle Morning for Real Estate Agents* coauthor, is an avid practitioner of the Life S.A.V.E.R.S. Part of Michael's morning routine is to write down his appreciations and affirmations in what he calls his Blessings Book. Michael says it best:

"What you appreciate ... APPRECIATES. It is time to take our insatiable appetite for what we want and replace it with an insatiable appetite and gratitude for what we do have. Write your appreciations, be grateful and appreciative, and you will have more of those things you crave—better relationships, more material goods, more happiness."

There is strength in writing down what you appreciate, and reviewing this material can change your mindset on a challenging day. A great practice to add to your routine is to write what you appreciate about your significant other, your child(ren), and especially yourself. When we write down the things we appreciate about our kids and spouse, even (and particularly) when they are not on their best behavior, it's easier to focus on their positive qualities. This is also a great step toward the activities we'll be sharing in section 2 of the book!

For example, you may be angry with your son because he hit

your daughter, but afterward he attempted to comfort her. Instead of focusing on his poor choice, be grateful for his compassion after the fact. Another example would be when your spouse is late for your date night. It would be easy to get angry, but instead, you can feel grateful that he arrived safely and that you're out of the house and away from the kids!

While there are many worthwhile benefits of keeping a daily journal, here are a few more of our favorites. With daily scribing, you'll:

- **Gain Clarity**—Journaling will give you more clarity and understanding of your past and current circumstances, help you work through challenges you're facing, and allow you to brainstorm, prioritize, and plan your actions each day to optimize your future.

- **Capture Ideas**—You will be able to capture, organize, and expand on your ideas while keeping the important ones you are saving for an opportune moment in the future.

- **Review Lessons**—Journaling provides a place to record, reference, and review the lessons you've learned, from both your wins and any mistakes you make along the way.

- **Acknowledge Your Progress**—Going back and rereading your journal entries from a year—or even a week—ago, and seeing how much progress you've made, can be hugely beneficial. It truly is one of the most enjoyable, eye-opening, and confidence-inspiring experiences, and it can't be duplicated any other way.

- **Improve Your Memory**—People always think they will remember things, but if you've ever gone to the grocery store without a list, you know this is simply untrue. When we write something down, we are much more likely to remember it, and if we forget, we can always go back and read it again.

Effective Journaling

Here are three simple steps to get started with journaling or improve your current journaling process.

First... Choose a format: physical or digital. You'll want to decide up front if you prefer a traditional, physical journal or a digital journal (on your computer or an app for your phone or tablet). If you aren't sure, experiment with both and see which feels best.

Second... Get a journal. Almost anything can work, but when it comes to a physical journal, there is something to be said for an attractive, durable one that you enjoy looking at—after all, ideally, you're going to have it for the rest of your life. We like to buy nice journals with lines on the pages, but it's your journal, so choose what works best for you. Some people prefer journals without lines, so they can draw or create mind maps. Others like to have one pre-dated page for each day of the year to help them stay accountable.

Here are a few favorite physical journals from TMM Facebook Community:

- *The Five-Minute Journal* (FiveMinuteJournal.com) has become popular among top performers. It has a very specific format for each day with prompts, such as "I am grateful for ..." and "What would make today great?" It takes five minutes or less and includes an evening option so you can review your day. This format is also wonderful for creating an appreciation for your partner!

- *The Freedom Journal* (TheFreedomJournal.com) gives you a

structured daily process that is focused on helping you with a single objective: *Accomplish Your #1 Goal in 100 Days*. Beautifully designed by John Lee Dumas of Entrepreneur On Fire, it's designed specifically to help you set and accomplish one big goal at a time.

- *The Plan: Your Legendary Life Planner* (TheLegendaryLife-Plan.com) was designed by Brandy, and it is a goal-setting and habit-tracking system and planner for people who are ready for life balance and are willing to be intentional about achieving level ten in all areas of life.

- *The Miracle Morning Journal* (MiracleMorningJournal.com) is designed specifically to enhance and support your Miracle Morning, to keep you organized and accountable, and to track your S.A.V.E.R.S. each day. You can also download a free sample of *The Miracle Morning Journal* today at TMMbook.com to make sure it's right for you.

If you prefer to use a digital journal, many choices are available. Here are a few favorites:

- *The Five-Minute Journal* (FiveMinuteJournal.com) also offers an iPhone app, which follows the same format as the physical version but allows you to upload photographs to your daily entries and sends you helpful reminders to input your entries each morning and evening.

- *Day One* (DayOneApp.com) is a popular journaling app, and it's perfect if you don't want any structure or any limits on how much you can write. Day One offers a blank page for each daily entry, so if you like to write lengthy journal entries, this may be the app for you.

- *Penzu* (Penzu.com) is a popular online journal that doesn't require an iPhone, iPad, or Android device. All you need is a computer.

Again, it really comes down to your preference and the features you want. If none of these digital options resonate with you, type "online journal" into Google, or simply type "journal" into the app store, and you'll get a variety of choices.

Third... Scribe daily. There are endless things you can write about—notes from the book you're reading, a list of things you're grateful for, and your top 3-5 priorities for the day are a good place to start. Write whatever makes you feel good and optimizes your day. Don't worry about grammar, spelling, or punctuation. Your journal is a place to let your imagination run wild, so keep a muzzle on your inner critic. Don't edit—just scribe!

Customizing Your S.A.V.E.R.S.

We know that you might have days when you can't do The Miracle Morning practice all at once. Feel free to split up the Life S.A.V.E.R.S. in any way that works for you. We want to share a few ideas specifically geared toward customizing the Life S.A.V.E.R.S. based on your schedule and preferences. Your current morning routine might allow you to fit in only a 6-, 20-, or 30-minute Miracle Morning, or you might choose to do a longer version on the weekends.

Here is an example of a common 60-minute Miracle Morning schedule using the Life S.A.V.E.R.S.:

Silence: 10 minutes

Affirmations: 5 minutes

Visualization: 5 minutes

Exercise: 10 minutes

Reading: 20 minutes

Scribing: 10 minutes

You can customize the sequence, too. Lance prefers to do a few jumping jacks to get his brain awake before he meditates. Brandy meditates before she leaves the bedroom for the rest of her Miracle Morning. Hal prefers to start with a period of peaceful, purposeful silence so that he can wake up slowly, clear his mind, and focus his energy and intentions. However, this is your Miracle Morning, not ours—feel free to experiment with different sequences to see which you like best.

Ego Depletion and Your Miracle Morning

Have you ever wondered why you can resist sugary snacks in the morning, but your resistance crumbles in the afternoon or evening? Why is it that sometimes our willpower is strong and other times it deserts us? It turns out that willpower is like a muscle that grows tired from use, and at the end of the day it is harder to push ourselves to do activities that serve us and avoid those that don't. It also means we have less patience for our loved ones in the afternoon and evening when they could probably use it the most.

The good news is that we know how this works and can set ourselves up for success with some advanced planning. And the great news? The Miracle Morning is an integral part of your plan. To see how this works, we need to understand ego depletion.

Ego depletion is a term to describe "a person's diminished capacity to regulate their thoughts, feelings, and actions," according to Roy F. Baumeister and John Tierney, the authors of *Willpower*. Ego depletion grows worse at the end of the day and when we are hungry, tired, or have had to exert our willpower too often.

If you wait until the end of the day to do important things that give you energy and help you become the person you want to be, you'll find that your excuses are more compelling, and your motivation has gone missing. But when you wake up and do your Miracle Morning first thing, you gain the increased energy and mindfulness that the Life S.A.V.E.R.S. provide and keep ego depletion from getting in your way.

When you perform the Life S.A.V.E.R.S. habit every day, you learn the mechanics of habit formation when your willpower is strongest, and you can use this knowledge and energy to adopt small and doable habits at other times of the day.

Final Thoughts on the Life S.A.V.E.R.S.

Everything is difficult before it's easy. Every new experience is uncomfortable before it's comfortable. The more you practice the Life S.A.V.E.R.S., the more natural and normal each of them will feel. Hal's first time meditating was almost his last because his mind raced like a Ferrari, and his thoughts bounced around uncontrollably like a pinball. Now, he loves meditation, and while he's still no master, he says he's decent at it.

Similarly, we had trouble with affirmations when we first started our Miracle Mornings. We didn't know what we wanted to affirm. So, we stole a few from *The Miracle Morning* and added a few that came to mind. It was okay, but they didn't really *mean* much to us initially. Over time, as we encountered things that struck us as powerful, we added them to our affirmations and adjusted the ones we had. Now, our affirmations mean a lot to us, and the daily act of using them is far more powerful.

In fact, we used the affirmation, "We are fully committed to writing *The Miracle Morning for Couples* this year by sticking to our deadlines and protecting time to write" to motivate ourselves daily to finish this very book!

We invite you to begin practicing the Life S.A.V.E.R.S. now, so you can become familiar and comfortable with each of them and get a jump-start before you begin The Miracle Morning 30-Day Challenge in section 4.

The Six-Minute Miracle Morning

If your biggest concern is still finding the time, don't worry; we've got you covered. You can do the entire Miracle Morning—receiving the full benefits of all six S.A.V.E.R.S.—in only six minutes a day, literally. While six minutes isn't the duration I'd recommend on an ongoing basis, for those days when you're pressed for time, simply do each of the S.A.V.E.R.S. for one minute each as follows:

Minute One (S): Close your eyes and enjoy a moment of peaceful, purposeful silence to clear your mind and get centered for your day.

Minute Two (A): Read your most important affirmation to reinforce *what* result you want to accomplish, *why* it's important to you, *which* specific actions you must take, and, most importantly, precisely *when* you will commit to taking those actions.

Minute Three (V): Visualize yourself flawlessly executing the single most important action that you want to mentally rehearse for the day.

Minute Four (E): Stand up and engage in some high-energy jumping jacks, or drop and do push-ups and/or crunches, to get your heart rate up and engage your physiology.

Minute Five (R): Grab the book you're reading and read a page (or a paragraph).

Minute Six (S): Grab your journal and jot down one thing that you're grateful for, along with the single most important result for you to generate that day.

We're sure you can see how, even in just six minutes, the S.A.V.E.R.S. will set you on the right path for the day—and you can always devote more time later when your schedule permits or the opportunity presents itself. Doing the six-minute practice is a way to start a mini habit to build up your confidence or a way to bookmark the habit on a tough morning. Another mini habit you could do is to start with one of the Life S.A.V.E.R.S. and, once you get used to waking up earlier, add more of them. Remember that the goal is to have some time to work on your personal goals and mindset, so if you are overwhelmed, it's not going to work for you.

Personally, our Miracle Morning has grown into a daily ritual of renewal and inspiration that we absolutely love! In the coming chapters, we will cover *a lot* of information (including an additional morning routine the two of you can do together!) that can turn you into a truly confident couple. We can't wait to share it with you.

SECTION II:
THE NOT-SO-OBVIOUS YOU PRINCIPLES

— 4 —
NOT-SO-OBVIOUS YOU
PRINCIPLE #1:
Self-Leadership

*"Your level of success will seldom exceed
your level of personal development…
because success is something you attract
by the person you become."*

—JIM ROHN, American entrepreneur, author,
and motivational speaker

What if the real secret to having more of what we want in our
lives is not about *doing* more but about *becoming* more.

It is this philosophy that gave birth to and remains the foundation of, The Miracle Morning: that our levels of success *in every single area of our lives* are always determined by our levels of *personal development* (i.e. our beliefs, knowledge, emotional intelligence, skills, abilities, faith, etc.). So, if we want to *have* more, we must first *become* more.

In other words, who you're becoming is far more important than what you're doing, and yet the irony is that what you're doing, each day, is determining who you're becoming.

Think of it this way: if you were to measure your desired level of success on a scale of one to ten, in every area of your life, it's safe to say that you want "level 10" success in each area. We've never met anyone who honestly said, "Nah, I don't want to be too happy, too healthy, or too wealthy…I am content just settling for less than my potential and cruising along with a level 5 life."

But what are we doing each day to first become a level 10 person and grow your You Element?

Andrew Bryant, the founder of Self-Leadership International, summed it up this way: "Self-leadership is the practice of intentionally influencing your thinking, feeling, and behaviors to achieve your objective(s) … [It] is having a developed sense of who you are, what you can do, and where you are going coupled with the ability to influence your communication, emotions, and behaviors on the way to getting there."

Before we reveal the key principles of self-leadership, we want to share with you what we've discovered about the crucial role that *mindset* plays as the foundation of effective self-leadership. Your past beliefs, self-image, and ability to collaborate with and rely upon others at integral times will factor into your ability to excel as a self-leader.

Be Aware—and Skeptical—of Your Self-Imposed Limitations

You may be holding on to false limiting beliefs that are unconsciously interfering with your ability to achieve your personal and professional goals.

For example, you may be someone who repeats, "I wish I were more organized." Yet you are more than capable of providing the structure and inspiration to be organized. Thinking of yourself as less than capable assumes imminent failure and simultaneously thwarts your ability to succeed. Life contains enough obstacles without your creating more for yourself!

Effective self-leaders closely examine their beliefs, decide which ones serve them, and eliminate the ones that don't.

When you find yourself stating anything that sounds like a limiting belief, from "I don't have enough time" to "I could never do that," pause and turn your self-limiting statements into empowering questions, such as the following: *Where can I find more time in my schedule? How might I be able to do that?*

Doing this allows you to tap into your inborn creativity and find solutions. You can always find a way when you're committed. As tennis star Martina Navratilova said, "The difference between involvement and commitment is like ham and eggs. The chicken is involved; the pig is committed." Being all in is the key to making anything happen.

See Yourself as Better than You've Ever Been

As Hal wrote in *The Miracle Morning*, most of us suffer from Rearview Mirror Syndrome, limiting our current and future results based on who we were in the past. Remember, although *where you are is a result of who you were, where you go depends entirely on the person you choose to be from this moment forward.* This is especially important for couples. You will make mistakes. Don't let your sense of guilt about that keep you from looking forward. Learn from your mistakes and do better next time.

Sara Blakely, the founder of Spanx and the youngest self-made female billionaire in the United States, attributes her success to a mindset her father instilled in her. "When I was growing up, he encouraged us to fail. We'd come home from school, and at dinner, he'd say, 'What did you fail at today?' And if there was nothing, he'd be disappointed. It was an interesting kind of reverse psychology. I would come home and say that I tried out for something and I was just horrible and he high-fived me." Our mistakes can turn into our greatest lessons.

We all make mistakes! As human beings, we do not come with instruction manuals, and there will always be someone with an unsolicited opinion about the way you are living your life. Don't listen to the static! Be confident in your choices, and when you aren't sure, find the answers and support you need.

All successful people, at some point, made the choice to see themselves as better than they had ever been before. They stopped maintaining limiting beliefs based on their past and instead started forming beliefs based on their unlimited potential.

One of the best ways to do this is to follow the four-step Miracle Morning Affirmations formula for creating results-oriented affirmations, as outlined in the last chapter. Be sure to create affirmations that reinforce what's possible for you by reminding you of your ideal outcome, why it's important to you, which actions you're committed to taking to achieve it, and precisely when you're committed to taking those actions.

Actively Seek Support

Seeking support is crucial for everyone, yet many struggle, suffering in silence because they assume everyone else has greater capabilities, and they all but refuse to seek help and assistance.

People who are self-leaders know they can't do it alone. You might need moral support, for example, so you can replenish the energy stores that life is so famous for depleting. Or you may need accountability support to overcome your tendency to disengage when the going gets tough. We all need support in different areas of our lives, and great self-leaders understand that and use it to their benefit.

The Miracle Morning Community on Facebook is a great place to start looking for support. The members are positive and responsive. You could also try joining a local group for people with similar goals and interests. Meetup.com is a great place to find like-minded folks who are close by. We highly recommend getting an accountability partner (or using your life partner as your accountability partner) and, if you can, a life or relationship coach to help you.

The Five Foundational Principles of Self-Leadership

While self-leadership is a skill, all skills are built on a foundation of principles. To grow and reach the levels of success you aspire to achieve, you'll need to become a proficient self-leader. Our favorite way to cut the learning curve in half and decrease the time it takes for you to reach the top one percent is to model the traits and behaviors of those who have reached the top before you.

Here are the five principles I believe will make the biggest impact on your commitment to self-leadership:

1. Take 100 Percent Responsibility/Emotional Intelligence

2. Prioritize Fitness and Make Exercise Enjoyable

3. Aim for Financial Freedom/Security

4. Systematize Your World

5. Commit to Your Result-Producing Process

Principle #1: Take 100 Percent Responsibility

Here's the hard truth: if your life and relationship are not where you want them to be, start by taking a hard look at yourself.

The sooner you take ownership of your own role, the sooner you'll begin to move forward. This isn't meant to be harsh. Successful people are rarely victims. In fact, one of the reasons they are successful is that they take absolute, total, and complete responsibility for each and every single aspect of their lives—whether it's personal or professional, good or bad, their job or someone else's.

While victims habitually waste their time and energy blaming others and complaining, achievers are busy creating the results and circumstances they want for their lives. They're so busy working on building a life they love that they don't have time to complain.

According to Hal, "The moment you take 100 percent responsibility for everything in your life is the same moment you claim your power to change anything in your life. However, the crucial distinction is to realize that taking responsibility is not the same thing as accepting *blame*. While blame determines who is at fault for something, responsibility determines who is committed to improving a situation. It rarely matters who is at fault. All that matters is that YOU are committed to improving your situation." He's right. And it's so empowering when you truly start to think and act accordingly. Suddenly, your life and your results are within your control.

When you take true ownership of your life, there's no time for discussing whose fault something is, or who gets the blame. Playing the blame game is easy, but there's no longer any place for it in your life. You own your results—good and bad. You can celebrate the good and learn from the so-called bad. Either way, you always have a choice about how you respond or react in any and every situation. This also applies to situations where you are triggered by your partner or kids.

One of the reasons this mindset is so important is that you are leading by example. If you're always looking for someone to blame, your partner sees that, and they likely don't respect it.

Here's the psychological shift we suggest you make: take ownership and stewardship over all of your decisions, actions, and outcomes, starting right now. Replace unnecessary blame with unwavering responsibility. Even if someone else drops that ball, ask yourself what you could have done, and, more importantly, what you can do in the future, to prevent it from happening again. While you can't change what's in the past, the good news is that you can change everything else.

From now on, there's no doubt about who is at the wheel and who is responsible for all your results. You make the calls, do the follow-up, decide the outcomes you want, and get the results. Your results are 100 percent your responsibility. Right?

Remember you are in control, and there are no limits to what you can accomplish.

Principle #2: Prioritize Fitness and Make Exercise Enjoyable

On a scale of one to ten, where would you rank your health and fitness? Are you fit? Strong? Do you *feel* good, more often than not?

How about your energy level throughout the day? Do you have more energy than you know what to do with? Can you wake up before your alarm and do what's important, handle all the demands of the day, and put out the inevitable fires, all without struggling to make it through the day without feeling exhausted and out of breath?

We covered exercise as the "E" in S.A.V.E.R.S., and yes, we're going to discuss it again right now. The state of your health and fitness is a huge factor in your energy and success levels—especially for couples.

It's no surprise, then, that three priorities of top performers, each of which you must prioritize in your life, are the quality of their food, their sleep, and their exercise. We'll delve deeper into each in the next chapter on *Energy Engineering*, but let's start with making sure you get your daily exercise in. The key is to find physical activities that you truly enjoy.

Make exercise enjoyable. The correlation between physical fitness, happiness, and success are undeniable. It is no coincidence that you rarely see top performers who are terribly out of shape. Most schedule and invest 30-60 minutes of their time each day to hit the gym or the running trail, because they understand the important role that daily exercise plays in their success.

While the "E" in S.A.V.E.R.S. ensures that you're going to start each day with 5-10 minutes of exercise, we recommended that you make a commitment to engage in additional 30-60-minute workouts, at least three to five times per week. Doing so will ensure that your fitness level supports the energy and confidence you need to succeed in your relationship and in your life.

Even better is to engage in some form of exercise that brings you a deep level of enjoyment. Whether that means going for a hike in nature, playing ultimate Frisbee, or putting an exercise bike in front of your TV so you can enjoy your favorite episode of *Breaking Bad* and forget that you're even exercising. Or, do what Hal does: he loves wakeboarding and playing basketball—two excellent forms of exercise—so he does one of them every single workday. You'll see Hal's foundational schedule in the coming pages to show you how those activities fit with the rest of his priorities.

Which physical activities do you enjoy, that you can commit to scheduling as part of your daily exercise ritual?

Principle #3: Aim for Financial Freedom/Security

How is your journey toward financial freedom looking? Are you earning significantly more money each month than you need to survive? Are you able to consistently save, invest, and contribute a significant portion of your income? Are you debt-free, with a large reserve that allows you to capitalize on opportunities that come your way and weather any unexpected financial storms? Are you on pace for financial freedom, so that your ongoing passive income will exceed your ongoing monthly expenses? If so, congratulations. You are among a very small percentage of couples who are genuinely thriving with their finances.

If not, you're not alone. Most people have less than $10,000 to their name, along with an average of $16,000 in unsecured debt. No judgment here if your finances are not yet where you want them to be; we're simply going to point you right back to the first principle and encourage you to take 100 percent responsibility for your financial situation.

We've seen and heard every reason for someone to dive deep into debt, fail to save, and not have a nest egg. None of those matter now. Yes, the best time to have started saving a percentage of your income was five, ten, or even twenty years ago. But the next best time is right now. Whether you're 20, 40, 60, or 80 years old, it's never too late to take control of your personal finances. You'll find an incredible boost in energy from taking charge, and you'll be able to use your accumulated savings to create even more wealth because you'll have money to invest in new opportunities. Sounds good, right?

Financial freedom isn't something you achieve overnight. It is a result of developing the mindset and the habits *now* that will take you down the path that leads to financial freedom. Here are 4.8 practical steps you can start taking today to ensure that you are aiming your financial habits toward a future of financial freedom:

1. **Set aside 10 percent of your income to save and invest.** This is a must. In fact, we recommend that you start by taking 10 percent of whatever funds you have in the bank right now and putting it into a separate savings account. (Go ahead, we'll wait.) Make whatever adjustments you need to make to your lifestyle to be able to live off 90 percent of your current income. A little discipline and sacrifice go a long way. Seeing that 10 percent add up over time gets exciting, and you'll start to *feel* what's possible for the future.

2. **Take another 10 percent and give it away.** Most wealthy people give a percentage of their income to causes they believe in. But you don't have to wait until you're wealthy to start this practice. Tony Robbins said, "If you won't give $1 out of $10, you'll never give $1 million out of $10 million." Can't do 10 percent or the rent check will bounce? Fine, start with 5, 2, or 1 percent. It's not the amount that matters but developing the mindset and creating the habit that will change your financial future and serve you for the rest of your life. You've got to start teaching your subconscious brain that it can produce an abundant income, that there's more than enough, and that there is always more on the way.

3. **Continually develop your money mindset.** It's one of the most important topics for you to master, and you can start by adding the following books, which cover various aspects of financial freedom, to your reading list:

   • *Profit First: A Simple System to Transform Any Business from a*

Cash-Eating Monster to a Money-Making Machine by Mike Michalowicz

- *Secrets of the Millionaire Mind: Mastering the Inner Game of Wealth* by T. Harv Ecker

- *The Total Money Makeover: A Proven Plan for Financial Fitness* by Dave Ramsey

- *The Millionaire Fastlane: Crack the Code to Wealth and Live Rich for a Lifetime* by MJ DeMarco

- *MONEY: Master the Game: 7 Simple Steps to Financial Freedom* by Anthony Robbins

- *Think and Grow Rich* by Napoleon Hill

- *Rich Dad Poor Dad* by Robert Kiyosaki

- *Magic Money: A Course in Creating Abundance* (books 1-3) by Holly Alexander

We want to point out that financial matters are the biggest source of fighting and arguments among couples. So no matter where you are on your journey of financial security, it is important to keep your partner in the loop. While it's not the most romantic—and is often quite a difficult—thing to talk about, continual discussion and checking in on finances will go a long way to mitigating heated discussions down the road.

Principle #4: Systematize Your World

Effective self-leaders have *systems* for just about everything, from work activities—such as scheduling, following up, entering orders, and sending thank you cards—to personal activities, such as sleeping, eating, and managing your money, home, and family responsibilities. Those systems make up your life.

Here are a few practices you can implement immediately to begin systematizing your world:

1. Automate What You Can

In our home, certain foods and household products are a necessity, and constantly needing to stop at the grocery store for replenishments became burdensome. We use a service that delivers groceries, so we decided to have them delivered to us instead of running out all the time for more. If you find something similar in your life that does not bring you joy, try to eliminate it through automation.

Another example is that we hate cleaning toilets and doing the laundry, so we found a way to hire help for those chores. One benefit is that it makes us accountable for keeping the house clutter-free. The housekeepers can do their job well only if things are up off the floor and surfaces. Sunday evening is pick-up time in our house. The whole family gets involved in getting the house ready. We realize housekeepers may not be in the budget for everyone, but if you can't yet afford one, you may be able to trade services with friends or come up with other creative solutions. One of our friends includes house cleaning as the exercise portion of the Life S.A.V.E.R.S., so a little gets done every morning

2. Briefcases and Beyond

Hal, in addition to being a bestselling author, is a speaker who travels week after week, sharing The Miracle Morning message with audiences around the country and abroad. Collecting the items he needed for every trip was time-consuming, inefficient, and ineffective because he would often forget something at home or in his office. After the third time he forgot the charger for his computer and had to find an Apple store to buy a $99 replacement (ouch) or had to ask the front desk for a phone charger, shaver, or extra set of cufflinks left behind by a previous guest, he'd had enough. He assembled a travel bag containing every item he needs for his trips, and now he can leave at a moment's notice because his bag contains everything to conduct business on the road: business cards, brochures, copies of his books, adapters, and chargers for his phone and computer. He even includes earplugs in case his hotel room neighbor is noisy.

You'll know you need a system when you have a recurring challenge or find that you're missing important items because you're unprepared. If you're walking out the door with just enough time to get to your first destination of the day on schedule only to discover your car is running on fumes, you need a system for getting out the door earlier. Here are some ways to plan ahead:

- Pack your lunch, your purse or briefcase, and your gym bag the night before, and lay out your outfit for the next day.

- If you have kids, have their stuff prepared the night before, too.

- Stash healthy snacks (apples, kale chips, carrots, etc.) for when you're on the go to prevent stopping at a convenience store or fast-food joint for a not-so-healthy option.

Said another way, wherever you need to get your act together, you need a system. A life without systems is a life with unnecessary stress! This is especially true for busy couples, especially when you have kids.

3. Foundational Scheduling

The use of a foundational schedule is key to maximizing

your focus, productivity, and income. If we spend too many days bouncing around from one task to another, we end far too many days wondering where in the hell the time went and what, if any, significant progress was made. We've missed more key opportunities than we can calculate. Can you relate?

We are going to share something that will transform your ability to produce consistent and spectacular results: *you must create a foundational schedule that gives structure and intentionality to your days and weeks.* A foundational schedule is a pre-determined, recurring schedule that is made up of focused time-blocks, each of which is dedicated to your highest priority activities. Most of us intuitively understand the benefits of this, but very few do it effectively on a consistent basis.

We know, we know—you were excited to get away from structure once you became an adult. Trust me, we get it. But the more you leverage a foundational schedule, consisting of time-blocks—typically ranging from one to three hours each—that are dedicated to focusing on the projects or activities that will help you make the most of your life and relationship—the more freedom you'll ultimately create.

That's not to say you cannot have flexibility in your schedule. In fact, we strongly suggest that you *schedule* flexibility. Plan plenty of time-blocks for family, fun, and recreation into your calendar. You could even go as far as to include a "whatever I feel like" time-block, during which you do, well ... whatever you feel like. You can also move things on occasion as needed. What's important is that you go through your days and weeks with a high level of intentionality about how you're going to invest every hour of every day, even if that hour is spent doing *whatever you feel like*. At least you planned on it. Maintaining a foundational schedule is how you will ensure that you maximize your productivity so that you almost never end the day wondering where in the hell your time went. Your day won't go anywhere without you making a conscious decision, because you'll be intentional with every minute of it.

We asked Hal to share his weekly foundational schedule, so you can see an example of what this can look like. Although Hal has the luxury of entrepreneurial freedom and doesn't need to follow any pre-determined schedule, he will tell you that having this foundational schedule in place is one of his keys to ensuring he maximizes each day.

Hal's Foundational Schedule

Time	Mon	Tues	Wed
4:00 AM	SAVERS	SAVERS	SAVERS
5:00 AM	Write	Write	Write
6:00 AM	Emails	Emails	Emails
7:00 AM	Take Kids to School	Take Kids to School	Take Kids to School
8:00 AM	Team Mtg.	#1 Priority	#1 Priority
9:00 AM	#1 Priority	Wakeboard	↓
10:00 AM	↓	↓	↓
11:00 AM	Lunch	Lunch	Lunch
12:00 PM	Basketball	Priorities	Basketball
1:00 PM	Priorities	Interview	Client Call
2:00 PM	Priorities	Interview	Client Call
3:00 PM	Priorities	Interview	Client Call
4:00 PM	Priorities	Priorities	Priorities
5:00 PM	FAMILY	FAMILY	FAMILY
9:00 PM	Bed	Bed	Bed

Time	Thurs	Fri	Sat/Sun
4:00 AM	SAVERS	SAVERS	SAVERS
5:00 AM	Write	Write	Write
6:00 AM	Emails	Emails	⬇
7:00 AM	Take Kids to School	Take Kids to School	FAMILY Time
8:00 AM	#1 Priority	#1 Priority	⬇
9:00 AM	Wakeboard	⬇	⬇
10:00 AM	⬇	⬇	⬇
11:00 AM	Lunch	Lunch	⬇
12:00 PM	Priorities	Basketball	⬇
1:00 PM	Interview	Priorities	⬇
2:00 PM	Interview	Priorities	⬇
3:00 PM	Interview	Priorities	⬇
4:00 PM	Priorities	PLANNING	⬇
5:00 PM	FAMILY	Date Night	⬇
9:00 PM	Bed	??? ☺	Bed

(Note: Every hour is planned)

Keep in mind that, like most everyone, things come up that cause Hal's foundational schedule to change (events, speaking engagements, vacations, etc.), but only temporarily. As soon as he's back home and in his office, this is the schedule that he falls back into.

One of the main reasons that this technique is so effective is because it takes the emotional roller coaster, caused by varied results, out of the decision-making for your daily activities. How many times has an appointment gone bad and then affected your emotional state and your ability to focus for the rest of the day? Chances are, your focus and productivity were hindered for the rest of that day. If you had followed your foundational schedule, though, and the calendar said, "networking event," "writing ads," or "making calls," and you were committed to the calendar, then you would have had a fruitful afternoon. Take control. Stop leaving your productivity up to chance and letting outside influences manage your calendar. Create your foundational schedule—one that incorporates everything you need to get done, as well as recreational, family and fun time—and follow through with it, no matter what. If you find you need additional support to ensure that you follow through, send a copy of your foundational schedule to an accountability partner or your coach, and have them hold you accountable. Your commitment to this one system will allow you to have significantly more control over your productivity and results.

Principle #5: Commit to Consistency

If there is any not-so-obvious secret to success, this is it: *commit to consistency*. Every result that you desire—from improving your physique to increasing the size of your business to spending more quality time with your family—requires a consistent approach to produce the desired results.

In the chapters that follow, we'll give you the insight and direction you need to take consistent action. For now, prepare your mind to keep going—even when the results you want aren't coming fast enough—and to have the stamina to withstand plenty of rejection and disappointment as you adjust to your new self. The happiest people are consistent, persistent, and unfailing in their dedication to taking action every day, and you need to be the same!

How is Your Self-esteem?

Self-esteem gives you the courage to try new things and the power to believe in yourself. As American playwright August Wilson suggests, "Confront the dark parts of yourself, and work to banish them with illumination and forgiveness. Your willingness to wrestle with your demons will cause your angels to sing."

It is vitally important that you give yourself permission to feel proud of yourself. Yes, we need to be realistic about our weaknesses and always strive to improve, but don't hesitate to be proud of your strengths and revel in the little wins. In the meantime, many days are filled with disappointments, delays, and denials, so it is vitally important that you love yourself. If you are doing the best you can, give yourself credit. We keep a special section in our journals to write love notes to ourselves. On days we need a little extra encouragement, we write down all the things we love and appreciate about ourselves.

Unstoppable self-esteem is a powerful tool. You probably already know that a negative attitude gets you nowhere—and fast! With the right attitude, all the challenges of the day can roll off your back. You stay calm and can keep going. When you are confident in your abilities and committed to consistency, your behavior will change, and your success is inevitable.

Putting Self-Leadership into Action

Let's review the concepts we discussed in this chapter. We talked about the importance of self-leadership in improving your life, both personally and professionally. Developing self-leadership helps put you in the leadership role of your life. It eliminates the victim mentality and ensures you know the values, beliefs, and vision you want to live into.

Step One: Review and integrate the Five Foundational Principles of Self-Leadership:

- **Take 100 Percent Responsibility.** Remember, the moment you accept responsibility for *everything* in your life is the moment you claim the power to change *anything* in your life. Your success is 100 percent up to you.

- **Prioritize Fitness and Make Exercise Enjoyable.** If daily fitness isn't already a priority in your life, make it so. In addition to your morning exercise, block time for longer, 30-60-minute workouts three to five times each week. Also, we'll cover which foods will give you a surplus of energy in the next chapter.

- **Aim for Financial Freedom.** Begin to develop the mindset and habits that will inevitably lead you to a life of financial freedom, including saving a minimum of 10 percent of your income, continuously educating yourself on the topic of money, and diversifying your sources of income.

- **Systematize Your World.** Start by creating a foundational schedule. Then identify which area of your life or business can benefit by you putting systems and time-blocked schedules in place so that your result-producing processes have been predetermined every day and your success is virtually guaranteed. Most importantly, make sure you instill some system for accountability into your world, whether that be through a colleague, a coach, or your partner.

- **Commit to Consistency.** Everyone needs structure. Choose consistency, and commit to personal expectations and values. If you're trying a new approach, give it an extended period to work before throwing in the towel to try something different.

Step Two: Develop your self-control and upgrade your self-image by using affirmations and visualization. Be sure to customize both at your earliest opportunity; it takes time to see results, and the sooner you start, the sooner you'll notice improvements.

By now, we hope you've gained a sense of how important your personal development is in creating success. As you continue to read this book—and we suggest you read it more than once—we recommend that you intentionally address the areas where you know you need improvement and expansion. If your self-esteem could use a boost, then take steps to elevate it. Design affirmations to increase and develop it over time. Visualize yourself acting with more confidence, raising your personal standards, and loving yourself more.

If this sounds overwhelming, remember the power of incremental change. You don't have to do everything all at once. And we've got more good news for you. In the next chapter, we're going to break down exactly how to engineer your life to create optimum levels of sustained physical, mental, and emotional energy so that you're able to maintain extraordinary levels of clarity, focus, and action, day in and day out.

— 5 —
NOT-SO-OBVIOUS YOU PRINCIPLE #2:
Energy Engineering

"The world belongs to the energetic."

—RALPH WALDO EMERSON, American essayist,
lecturer, philosopher, and poet

We live and die by our own steam. Most of the time, if you don't
have energy, *you don't enjoy your life.* On some days—and we know
you've had those days—you wake up and just don't have the energy
or motivation you need to meet the challenges you know are coming.
Life can be exhausting, both physically and mentally. Maintaining
your focus on those days, amid uncertainty and overwhelm, is no
easy task. The good days take energy, enthusiasm, and persistence.

The hard days take all that and more.

A person with low energy suffers greatly. Motivation is hard to sustain. The focus is often generated artificially by stimulants, such as by drinking coffee all day long. *A legendary life requires an abundance of energy.* There's no way around it. You can have the best action plan for the day, but if you don't have the *energy* to get it done, reaching your goals is going to be unnecessarily difficult. If you want to maximize your life, you need energy—the more, the better, and the more *consistent,* the better.

- Energy is the fuel that enables you to maintain clarity, focus, and action so that you can generate stellar results, day after day.

- Energy is contagious; it spreads from you to the world around you like a positive virus, creating symptoms of enthusiasm and positive responses everywhere.

- Energy is the foundation of everything, and it is what determines the success we attract.

The question is, *how do you strategically engineer your life to so that you maintain a high level of sustainable energy*, which is always available to you, on demand?

When we struggle with energy issues, we might try to compensate with caffeine and other stimulants, and they'll work for a while … until we crash. You may have noticed the same thing. You can lean on stimulants to build up energy for a short while, but then the energy seems to fall off just when you need it the most.

If you've been fueling yourself on coffee and pure determination, you haven't even begun to reach the heights of achievement that are possible when you understand how energy works and commit to engineering your life for optimum energy.

Natural Energy Cycles

The first thing to understand about energy is that the goal isn't to be running at full speed all the time. It isn't practical to maintain a constant output. As human beings, we have a natural ebb and flow to our energy levels. Being the best You, it turns out, is the same. Know that you will need to access deeper wells of energy during particularly intense times throughout the year and allow yourself the time to rest, rejuvenate, and recharge when the intensity lessens.

Just like houseplants need water, our energy reserves need regular replenishing. You can go full tilt for long periods, but eventually your mind, body, and spirit will need to be refilled. Think of your life as a container that holds your energy. When you do not properly manage what's in your container, it's like having a hole in the bottom. No matter how much you pour in, you still won't feel fully energized. Rachel Hollis gives the example of the difference between what most of us do—pouring our vase of water out to give to everything else before ourselves—and what we should do—pour into ourselves, so our vase flows over so much that it gives to everyone around us.

Instead of letting yourself get to the point of being overwhelmed, burned out, or stressed out, why not become proactive about your energy levels and have an auto-recharge system in place? This will help you plug the holes in your container and allow you to fill up with the energy you need.

If you have resigned yourself to being tired, cranky, behind on your to-do list, out of shape, and unhappy, I have some great news.

Being continually exhausted is not only unacceptable, *you don't have to settle for it.* There are a few simple ways to get what you need and want: more rest, time to replenish and recharge, and inner peace and happiness. A tall order? Yes. Impossible? Heck, no!

This is about strategically engineering your life for optimum and sustainable physical, mental, and emotional energy. Here are the three principles I follow to keep my energy reserves at maximum capacity and on tap for whenever I need them.

1. Eat and Drink for Energy

When it comes to energy engineering, what you eat and drink may play the most critical role of all. If you're like most people, you base your food choices on taste first and the consequences second (if you consider them at all). Yet, what pleases our taste buds in the moment doesn't always give us maximum energy to last throughout the day.

There is nothing wrong with eating foods that taste good, but if you want to be truly healthy and have the energy to perform like a champion, here's the big idea: it is crucial that we make a conscious decision to *place more value on the health and energy consequences of food than we do on the taste.* Why? Because digesting food is one of the most energy-draining processes that the body endures. Need evidence? Just take a second to think about how exhausted you feel after a big meal (see: Thanksgiving dinner). It's no coincidence that a large meal is usually followed by heavy eyes and ultimately a nap. They call it a "food coma" for a reason.

Items like bread, dairy products, and any foods that have been processed require more energy to digest than they contribute to your body. So, rather than giving you energy, these essentially "dead" foods tend to drain your energy to fuel digestion and leave you in an energy deficit. On the other hand, "living" foods like raw fruits, vegetables, healthy fats, protein, nuts, and seeds typically give you more energy than they require for digestion, thus empowering your body and mind with an energy surplus, which enables you to perform at your best.

Put very simply, everything you bring into your body either contributes to or detracts from your health and energy. Drinking water puts a check in the plus column; double shots of tequila drain your health and energy. Eating a diet rich with fresh fruits and vegetables equals more pluses. Rolling through the drive-through to wolf down some fast food? Not so much. I know you know the drill. This isn't rocket science, but it may be the single most important area of your life to optimize. You may need to stop fooling yourself.

If you're not already doing so, it's time to be intentional and strategic about what you eat, when you eat, and, most importantly, *why* you eat so that you can engineer your life for optimum energy.

Strategic Eating

Up until this point, you may have been wondering, *when the heck do I get to eat during my Miracle Morning?* I'll cover that here. We'll also address *why* your choice to eat what you eat may be the most important consideration of all.

When To Eat—Again, remember that digesting food is one of the most energy-draining processes the body goes through each day. The bigger the meal, the more food you give your body to digest, the more drained you will feel. With that in mind, we recommend eating your first meal *after* your Miracle Morning. This ensures that, for optimum alertness and focus during the S.A.V.E.R.S., your blood will be flowing to your brain rather than to your stomach to digest your food.

However, we do recommend starting your day by ingesting a small amount of healthy fat, as fuel for your brain. Studies show that keeping your mind sharp and your moods in balance may be largely related to the type of fat you eat. "Our brain is at least 60 percent fat, and it's composed of fats (like omega-3s) that must be obtained from the diet," says Amy Jamieson-Petonic, MEd, a registered dietitian, the director of wellness coaching at the Cleveland Clinic, and a national spokesperson for the American Dietetic Association.

After drinking our first full glass of water, we start every morning with a tablespoon of organic coconut butter (specifically *Nutiva Organic Coconut Manna*, which you can order from Amazon.com), collagen protein powder, and a large mug of organic coffee, which we blend with Bulletproof Cacao Butter (available on Bulletproof.com). The tablespoon of coconut butter is such a small amount that it's easily digested and contains healthy fats to provide fuel for the brain. And the health benefits of cacao are significant, from being a powerhouse full of antioxidants (cacao rates in the top 20 on the oxygen radical absorbance capacity, a.k.a. "ORAC" scale, which is used to rate the antioxidant capacity of foods) to lowering blood pressure.

Maybe the most exciting benefit is that eating cacao makes you happy! It contains phenylethylamine (known as the "love drug"), which is responsible for our state of mood, pleasure and delivers the same feelings you get when you are in love. It also acts as a stimulant and can improve mental alertness. In other words, cacao = win, win, win!

If you do feel like you must eat a meal first thing in the morning, make sure that it's a small, light, easily digestible meal, such as fresh fruit or a smoothie (more on that in a minute).

Why To Eat—Let's take a moment to delve deeper into *why* you choose to eat the foods that you do. When you're shopping at the grocery store or selecting food from a menu at a restaurant, what criteria do you use to determine which foods you are going to put into your body? Are your choices based purely on taste? Texture? Convenience? Are they based on health? Energy? Dietary restrictions?

Most people eat the foods they do based mainly on the *taste* and, at a deeper level, on the emotional attachment to the foods they like the taste of. What would happen if you asked someone, "Why did you eat that ice cream? Why did you drink that soda?" Or, "Why did you bring that fried chicken home from the grocery store?" You would most likely hear responses like, "Mmm, because I love ice cream! ... I like drinking soda. ... I was in the mood for fried chicken." All of these answers are based on the emotional enjoyment derived primarily from the way these foods taste. In this case, this person is not likely to explain their food choices by how much value these foods will add to their health or how much sustained energy they'll receive as a result of ingesting them.

The point is this: if we want to have more energy (which we all do) and if we want our lives to be healthy and disease-free (which we all do), then it is crucial that we re-examine why we eat the foods that we do. From this point forward—and I know we've covered this, but it bears repeating—*start placing significantly more value on the health and energy consequences of the foods you eat than you do on the taste.* The taste only provides you with a few minutes of pleasure, but the health and energy consequences impact not only the rest of your day but the rest of your life.

Remember the old saying, *you are what you eat?* Take care of your body so your body will take care of you. You will feel vibrant energy and enhanced clarity immediately!

Again, in no way are we saying that we should eat foods that don't taste good in exchange for the health and energy benefits. We are saying that we can have both. If we want to live every day with an abundance of energy so we can perform at our best and live long, healthy lives, we must choose to eat more foods that are good for our health and give us sustained energy, as well as taste great.

We have shifted our view of food from that of a reward, treat, or comfort to that of fuel. We want to eat delicious, healthy foods that boost our energy levels and allow us to keep going as long as we need to go.

Honestly, sometimes we still enjoy certain foods that are not the healthiest choices, but we strategically reserve them for times when we don't need to maintain optimum energy levels, such as in the evenings and on weekends.

How to Make Better Food Decisions

The easiest way for us to make better decisions about our eating was to pay attention to the way we felt after eating certain foods. We set a timer for sixty minutes after we finished each meal. When the timer went off, we assessed our energy levels. It didn't take long for us to recognize which foods gave us the biggest power boost and which ones didn't. We can clearly tell the difference in our energy levels on the days when we drink a smoothie or eat a salad, and the days we cave for a chicken sandwich or some of that pizza that smells so good. The former gives us a surplus of energy, while the latter puts us in an energy deficit.

What would it be like to give your body what it needs to work and play for as long as you'd like? What would it be like to give yourself exactly what you truly deserve? Give yourself the gift of great health, consciously chosen through what you eat and drink.

If you are eating throughout the day almost as an afterthought, maybe hitting a drive-through after you've reached the point of being famished, it is time to start building a new strategy.

Give some thought to the following:

- Can I start to consciously consider the consequences of what I eat (both in health and energy) and value those above the taste?

- Can I keep water with me so that I can hydrate with intention and purpose and avoid becoming dehydrated?

- Can I plan my meals in advance, including incorporating healthy snacks, so I can combat any patterns I have that don't serve me?

Yes, you can do all of these and much more. Think about how much better your life will be and how much more energy you will have for your business when you become conscious and intentional about your eating and drinking habits.

- You will easily maintain a positive mental and emotional state. Low energy causes us to feel down, whereas high energy levels produce a positive state of mind, outlook, and attitude.

- You will be more disciplined. Low energy drains our will-power, making us more likely to choose to do the *easy* things over the *right* things. High energy levels increase our level of self-discipline.

- You will live longer.

- You will set an example for the people you lead and the people you love. How we live our lives gives permission to those around us to do the same.

- You will get healthier, feel much better, and live longer.

- Bonus—You will settle at your natural weight effortlessly.

In the end, here is the simple thing to remember: food is fuel. We should use it to get us from the beginning of the day all the way to the end, feeling great and having plenty of energy. Placing more value on the energy consequences of the foods you eat above the taste, along with eating foods that fuel energy, is the first step in energy engineering.

2. Sleep and Wake to Win

Sleep more to achieve more. That might be the most counter-intuitive business mantra you'll ever hear, but it's true. The body needs enough shut-eye each night to function properly and to recharge after a demanding day. Sleep also plays a critical role in immune function, metabolism, memory, learning, and other vital bodily functions. It's when the body does most of its repairing, healing, resting, and growing.

If you don't sleep enough, you're gradually wearing yourself down.

Sleeping Versus Sleeping *Enough*

How much sleep is enough? There is a big difference between the amount of sleep you can get by on and the amount you need to function optimally. Researchers at the University of California, San Francisco, discovered that some people have a gene that enables them to do well on six hours of sleep a night. This gene, however, is very rare, appearing in less than 3 percent of the population. For the other 97 percent of us, six hours doesn't come close to cutting it. Just because you're able to function on five to six hours of sleep doesn't mean you wouldn't feel a lot better and get more done if you spent an extra hour or two in bed.

That may sound counterintuitive. We can almost hear you thinking, *spend more time in bed and get more done? How does that work?* But it has been well-documented that enough sleep allows the body to function at higher levels of performance. You'll not only work better and faster, but your attitude will improve, too.

If you're like most people, when you don't get enough rest you have difficulty concentrating, thinking clearly, and even remembering things. You might notice your ineffectiveness at home or at work or even blame these missteps on your busy schedule. The more sleep you miss, the more pronounced your symptoms become.

Also, a lack of rest and relaxation can really work a number on your mood. It is a scientific fact that when individuals miss out on good nightly rest, their personalities are affected, and they are generally grumpier, less patient, and more apt to snap at people. The result of missing out on critical, much-needed rest might make you a bear to be around, which is not much fun for anyone, yourself included.

Most adults cut back on their sleep to pack more activities into their day. As you run against the clock to beat deadlines, you might be tempted to skimp on sleep to get more done. Unfortunately, lack of sleep can cause the body to run down, which allows illnesses, viruses, and diseases the tiny opening they need to attack the body. When you are sleep deprived, your immune system can become compromised and susceptible to just about anything. Eventually, lack of rest can cause illness that leads to missed days or even weeks of work.

On the flip side, when you get enough sleep, your body runs as it should, you're pleasant to be around, and your immune system is stronger. And that's precisely when you'll create more calmness and react more wisely around your partner and family. Think of good sleep as the time when you turn on your inner magnet.

How Much Sleep Do We *Really* Need?

The first thing experts will tell you about how many hours of sleep we need is that there is no universal number. The ideal duration of sleep varies from person to person and is influenced by factors such as age, genetics, stress, overall health, how much exercise a person gets, our diet—including how late we eat our last meal—and countless other factors. For example, if your diet consists of fast food, processed foods, excessive sugar, etc., then your body will be challenged to recharge and rejuvenate while you sleep, as it will be working all night to detoxify and filter out the poisons that you've put into it. On the other hand, if you eat a clean diet made up of living food, as we covered in the last section, then your body will recharge and rejuvenate much more easily. The person who eats a clean diet will almost always wake to feel refreshed, with more energy, and able to function optimally, even from less sleep, than the person who eats poorly.

We have been conditioned to think we need eight to ten hours of sleep, but according to the National Sleep Foundation, some research has found that long sleep durations (nine hours or more) are also associated with increased morbidity (illness, accidents) and even mortality (death). This research also found that variables such as depression were significantly associated with long sleep.

The amount of nightly rest each individual needs differs, but research shows that the average adult needs approximately seven to eight hours of sleep to restore the energy it takes to handle all of the demands of living each day.

Sometimes we need less sleep, and sometimes we need more. The best way to figure out if you're meeting your sleep needs is to evaluate how you feel as you go about your day. If you're logging enough hours, you'll feel energetic and alert all day long, from the moment you wake up until your regular bedtime. If you're not, you'll reach for caffeine or sugar mid-morning or mid-afternoon ... or both.

The True Benefits of Sleep

You may not realize how powerful sleep truly is. While you're happily wandering through your dreams, sleep is doing some hard work on your behalf and delivering a host of amazing benefits.

Sleep can help improve your memory. Your mind is surprisingly busy while you snooze. During sleep, you clean out damaging toxins that are byproducts of brain function during the day, strengthen memories, and practice skills learned while you were awake, all through a process called consolidation.

"If you are trying to learn something, whether it's physical or mental, you learn it to a certain point with practice, but something happens while you sleep that makes you learn it better," says Dr. David Rapoport, who is an associate professor at NYU Langone Medical Center as well as a sleep expert.

In other words, if you're trying to learn something new, whether it's Spanish, a new tennis swing, or the languages of love to help you improve communications with your partner, you'll perform better when you get adequate sleep.

Sleep can help you live longer. Too much or too little sleep is associated with a shorter life span, although it's not clear if it's a cause or an effect. In a 2010 study of women aged 50-79, more deaths occurred in women who got fewer than five hours or more than six-and-a-half hours of sleep per night. Getting the right amount of sleep is a good idea for your long-term health.

Sleep can help you be more creative. Log a good night's sleep before getting out the easel and paintbrushes or the pen and paper. In addition to consolidating memories or making them stronger, your brain appears to reorganize and restructure them, which may result in more creativity as well.

Researchers at Harvard University and Boston College found that people seem to strengthen the emotional components of memories during sleep, which may help spur the creative process.

Sleep can help you reach and maintain a healthy weight more easily. If you're overweight, you won't have the same energy levels as those at a healthy weight. If you are changing your lifestyle to include more exercise and diet changes, you'll want to plan an earlier bedtime. Putting additional physical demands on your body means you will need to counter-balance those demands with enough rest.

The good news: researchers at the University of Chicago found that dieters who were well-rested lost up to 56 percent more fat than those who were sleep-deprived, who lost more muscle mass. Dieters in the study also felt hungrier when they got less sleep. Sleep and metabolism are controlled by the same sectors of the brain, and when you are sleepy, the hormones that drive appetite increase in your blood.

Sleep can help you feel less stressed. When it comes to our health, stress, and sleep are closely connected, and both can affect cardiovascular health. Sleep can reduce stress levels, and with that comes better control of blood pressure. It is also believed that sleep affects cholesterol levels, which play a significant role in heart disease.

Sleep helps you avoid mistakes and accidents. The National Highway Traffic Safety Administration reported in 2009 that being tired accounted for the highest number of fatal, single-car, run-off-the-road crashes due to the driver's performance—even more than alcohol! Sleepiness is grossly underrated as a problem by most people, but the cost to society is enormous. Lack of sleep affects reaction time and decision-making abilities.

If insufficient sleep for only one night can be as detrimental to your driving ability as having an alcoholic drink, imagine how it affects your ability to maintain the focus necessary to rekindle your love life.

So, how many hours of sleep do you *really* need? You tell me, because only you truly know how much sleep you need to hit home run after home run. Now, if you really struggle with falling or staying asleep, and it is a concern for you, I highly recommend getting a copy of Shawn Stevenson's book, *Sleep Smarter: 21 Proven Tips to Sleep Your Way to a Better Body, Better Health, and Bigger Success.* It's one of the best-written and most-researched books that I've seen on the topic of sleep.

Getting consistent and effective rest is as critical to performing at your best as what you do or don't have in your diet. A good night's sleep provides the basis for a day of clear thought, sustained energy, and peak performance. You probably already know how many hours you need to be at your best, and it's important that you are optimizing your sleep. However, what may be even more important than how many hours of sleep you get each night may be how you approach the act of waking up in the morning.

You Snooze, You Lose: The Truth About Waking Up

The old saying, "you snooze, you lose," may have a much deeper meaning than any of us realized. When you hit the snooze button and delay waking up until you *must*—meaning you wait until the time when you have to be somewhere, do something, or take care of someone else—consider that you're starting your day with resistance. Every time you hit the snooze button, you're in a state of resistance to your day, to your life, and to waking up and creating the life you say you want.

According to Robert S. Rosenberg, medical director of the Sleep Disorders Centers of Prescott Valley and Flagstaff, Arizona, "When you hit the snooze button repeatedly, you're doing two negative things to yourself. First, you're fragmenting what little extra sleep you're getting, so it is of poor quality. Second, you're starting to put yourself through a new sleep cycle that you aren't giving yourself enough time to finish. This can result in persistent grogginess throughout the day."

If you're not already, make sure you start following the Five-Step Snooze-Proof Wake-Up Strategy, and you'll be poised to win. If getting to bed on time is your challenge, try setting a "bedtime alarm" that sounds an hour before your ideal bedtime, prompting you to start winding down so you can hit the sack.

On the other hand, when you wake up each day with passion and purpose, you join the small percentage of high achievers who are living their dreams. Most importantly, you will be happy. By simply changing your approach to waking up in the morning, you will literally change everything. But don't take my word for it—trust these famous early risers: Oprah Winfrey, Tony Robbins, Bill Gates, Rachel Hollis, Deepak Chopra, Wayne Dyer, Brian Johnson, Mel Robbins, Benjamin Franklin, Albert Einstein, Aristotle, and far too many more to list here.

No one ever taught us that by learning how to consciously set our intention to wake up each morning with a genuine desire—even enthusiasm—to do so, we can change our entire lives.

If you're just snoozing every day until the last possible moment you have to head off to work, show up for school, or take care of your family, and then zoning out at the end of the day in front of the television until you go to bed, we've got to ask you: *When are you going to develop into the person you need to be to create the health, wealth, happiness, success, and freedom that you truly want and deserve? When are you going to actually live your life instead of numbly going through the motions looking for every possible distraction to escape reality? What if your reality—your life—could finally be something that you can't wait to be conscious for?*

There is no better day than today for us to give up who we've been for who we can become and to upgrade the life we've been living for the one we really want. There is no better book than the one you are holding in your hands to show you how to become the person you need to be, the one who is capable of quickly attracting, creating and sustaining the life you have always wanted.

How To Wake Up With More Energy (On *Less* Sleep)

Since there is such a wide variety of opposing evidence from countless studies and experts, and since the amount of sleep needed varies from person to person, we're not going to attempt to make a case that there is one right approach to sleep. Instead, we'll share our real-world results, from personal experience and experimentation, as well as studying the sleep habits of some of the greatest minds in history. We'll warn you, though, some of this may be somewhat controversial.

Through experimenting with various sleep durations—as well as learning those of many other Miracle Morning practitioners who have tested this theory—Hal found that how our sleep affects our biology is largely impacted by our own personal *belief* about how much sleep we need. In other words, how we feel when we wake up in the morning is not solely based on how many hours of sleep we got but significantly impacted by how we told ourselves we were going to feel when we woke up—and this is a very important distinction.

For example, if you *believe* that you need eight hours of sleep to feel rested, but you're getting into bed at midnight and have to wake up at 6:00 a.m., you're likely to tell yourself, "Geez, I'm only going to get six hours of sleep tonight, but I need eight. I'm going to feel exhausted in the morning." Then, what happens as soon as your alarm clock goes off and you open your eyes and realize it's time to wake up? What's your first thought? It's the same thought you had before bed! "Geez, I only got six hours of sleep. I feel exhausted." It's a self-fulfilling, self-sabotaging prophecy. If you tell yourself you're going to feel tired in the morning, then you are absolutely going to feel tired. If you believe that you need eight hours to feel rested, then you're not going to feel rested on anything less. But what if you changed your beliefs?

The mind-body connection is a powerful thing, and we believe we must take responsibility for every aspect of our lives, including the power to wake up every day feeling energized, regardless of how many hours of sleep we get.

So, how many hours of sleep do you *really* need? You tell us.

3. Rest to Recharge

The conscious counterpart to sleep is *rest*. While some people use the terms interchangeably, they're quite different. You might get eight hours of sleep, but if you spend all of your waking hours on the go, then you won't have any time to think or recharge your physical, mental, and emotional batteries. When you work all day, run from activity to activity after hours, and then finish with a quick dinner and a late bedtime, you don't allow for a period of rest.

Likewise, spending weekends taking the kids to soccer, volleyball, or basketball, then heading out to see a football game, going to church, singing in the choir, attending several birthday parties, etc., can do more harm than good. While each of these activities is great, maintaining a fully packed schedule doesn't allow for time to recharge.

We live in a culture that perpetuates the belief that when our days are busy and exciting, we are more valuable, more important, or more alive. In truth, we are all of those things when we can be at peace within our own skin. Despite our best intentions to live balanced lives, the modern world demands that we are almost always connected and productive, and these demands can drain us emotionally, spiritually, and physically.

What if, instead of being constantly on the go, you valued intentional quiet time, sacred space, and periods of purposeful silence? How might that improve your life, your physical and emotional well-being, and your ability to achieve relationship happiness?

It may seem counterintuitive to take time out when your to-do list is a mile long, but the fact is that more rest is a prerequisite to truly productive work.

Research proves that rest melts your stress away. Practices like yoga and meditation also lower heart rates, blood pressure, and oxygen consumption while alleviating hypertension, arthritis, insomnia, depression, infertility, cancer, and anxiety. The spiritual benefits of resting are profound. Slowing down and getting quiet means you can actually hear your own wisdom, your inner knowledge, and your inner voice. Rest—along with its close sibling, relaxation—allows us to reconnect with the world in and around us, inviting ease and a sense of contentment into our lives.

And yes, in case you're wondering, you'll be more productive, nicer to your friends and family members (not to mention your partner), and in general much happier as well. When we rest, it's like letting the earth lay fallow rather than constantly planting and harvesting. Our personal batteries need to be recharged. The best way to recharge them is to truly and simply rest.

Easy Ways to Rest

Most of us confuse rest with recreation. To rest we do things like hike, garden, work out, or even party. Any of these activities can only be termed restful because they are breaks from work, but truthfully, they are not—and cannot be defined as—rest.

Rest has been defined as a kind of waking sleep, experienced while you are alert and aware. Rest is the essential bridge to sleep, and we achieve rest and sleep the same way: by making space for them and allowing them to happen. Every living organism needs rest, including you. When we don't take the time to rest, eventually its absence takes a toll on the body. Following are a few ideas to get some much-needed rest.

- If you are now investing five or ten minutes each morning, during your S.A.V.E.R.S., to meditate or sit in silence, that is a great start.

- You can reserve Sundays for rest, or, if Sunday is a busy workday for you, choose another day of the week.

- Read, watch a movie, do something low-key with family, or even spend time alone.

- Try cooking at home, playing games with your kids, and enjoying your loved ones' company.

- When you're driving, drive in silence: turn off the radio and stow your phone.

- Go for a walk without your earbuds. Even a walk in nature without intention or goals, such as burning calories, can work.

- Turn off the television. Designate a half hour, an hour, or even half a day for silence. Try taking a few conscious breaths, during which you focus on either the inhale and exhale or the space between breaths.

- You can also drink a cup of tea, read something inspirational, write in your journal, take a hot bath, or get a massage.

- Attend a retreat. It could be with your partner, a group of friends, your church, any community with which you are involved, family, or on your own in nature.

Even taking a nap is a powerful way to rest and recharge. If we're feeling drained during the day for some reason and still have a long day ahead, we won't hesitate to hit the reset button with a twenty- or thirty-minute power nap. Napping can also lead to better sleep patterns.

Set a specific time for rest. Put boundaries around it so you can claim that time.

The Rest Habit

You'll need to schedule your time for rest and self-care in the same way you schedule the other appointments in your life. The energy you get back will reward you many times over.

Rest certainly isn't something we were taught in school, and it may not come naturally at first. You may find that you need to consciously make it a priority. Learning different mindfulness practices and bringing them into your everyday life is an effective way to deeply rest your body, mind, and spirit. Practices such as mid-day meditation, yoga, and purposeful silence are powerful ways to go within and achieve restful states of being, particularly when you commit to practicing them regularly.

The more you integrate periods of rest and silence into your daily life, the bigger the payoff will be. During more tranquil periods, perhaps you won't need to rest as much, but periods of intensity (such as meeting a huge quota or a big deadline) may require more rest and silence than usual.

Combining exercise, healthy food choices, consistent sleep, and rest will give you a quantum leap in the right direction for you and your relationship. Keep in mind that when you try to adopt these three practices—eating, sleeping, and resting more effectively—you may at first find them to be uncomfortable. Your mind and body may encounter some emotional resistance. Resist the urge to run from the discomfort by making a commitment to begin putting them into practice, today.

Putting Energy Engineering into Action

Step One: Commit to eating and drinking for energy. Do this by prioritizing the energy consequences of the foods you eat above the taste. After your initial glass of water in the morning, ingest some form of healthy fat to fuel your brain. Try incorporating one new healthy meal, made up of *living* foods, into your diet each day. Instead of snacking on potato chips, try kale chips, or fresh organic fruit. And remember to keep a full bottle of water with you all the time to stay hydrated.

Step Two: Sleep and wake to win by choosing a consistent daily bedtime *and* wake-up time. Based on when you plan to wake for your Miracle Morning, back into a bedtime that ensures you will get enough sleep. Maintain a specific bedtime for a few weeks to get your body acclimated. If you need a little nudge to get to bed on time, set a bedtime alarm that prompts you to start winding down one hour before bedtime. After a couple of weeks, feel free to play with the number of hours you leave for sleeping to optimize your energy levels.

Step Three: Incorporate time into your daily calendar to rest and recharge, whether that involves meditation, a nap, going for a walk, or doing an activity that brings you joy. Remember, Hal takes a two-hour lunch break every day, which gives him time to either play basketball or wakeboard—two activities that he loves to do and that thoroughly reenergize him. Which activities can plan into your day that will reenergize you? In addition to your Miracle Morning routine, schedule regular daily periods to rest and recharge.

Now that you have a plan for your body let's direct our attention to focus.

— 6 —
NOT-SO-OBVIOUS YOU
PRINCIPLE #3:

Unwavering Focus

*"The successful warrior is the average man,
with laser-like focus."*

—BRUCE LEE, world-renowned martial artist and actor

We've all met that person. You know—*that* person. The one who runs marathons, coaches little league, volunteers at her son's school lunch program, is an incredible wife, and maybe writes a novel on the side. We bet you know someone like that—someone who just seems unexplainably productive.

Or maybe you know *this* person: the husband who's fit, always happy, and makes every person he encounters feel like a million bucks.

What you might not realize, though, is exactly how they do it. Maybe you always thought they were lucky. Or gifted. Or connected. Or had the right personality. Or were born with superpowers!

We know from experience that the real superpower behind every unbelievably productive, happy person is *unwavering focus*. Unwavering focus is the ability to maintain clarity about your highest priorities while taking all the energy you've learned to generate for yourself, channeling it into what matters most, and keeping it there, regardless of what is going on around you or how you feel. This ability is key to becoming an exceptional performer.

When you harness the power of focus, you don't become superhuman, but you can achieve seemingly superhuman results. And the reasons for this are surprisingly straightforward.

- **Unwavering focus makes you more effective.** Being effective doesn't mean doing the most things or doing things the fastest. It means doing the *right* things. You engage in the activities that create forward momentum toward your life's goals.

- **Unwavering focus makes you more efficient.** Being efficient means taking action with the fewest resources, such as time, energy, or money. Every time your mind wanders away from your goals, you waste those assets—particularly time. In pursuit of our goals, time is always in demand, so each moment that your focus wavers is another moment lost.

- **Unwavering focus makes you productive.** Understand that just because you're *busy* does not mean you're productive. In fact, struggling and disconnected couples are usually some of the busiest. Too often we confuse being busy—engaged in activities that don't produce results, like checking emails or cleaning your car or reorganizing your to-do list for the twelfth time this month—with being productive. When you have a clear vision, identify your highest priorities, and consistently execute your most-leveraged activities, you'll go from being busy to being productive. By taking the steps that we're about to cover, you'll learn how to develop the habit of unwavering focus and join the ranks of the most productive people in the world.

If you combine those benefits, you will achieve *a lot* more. Perhaps the greatest value of focus, however, is that rather than scattering your energy across multiple areas of your life and getting mediocre results across the board, you will release untapped potential *and* improve your life.

Now let's turn your Miracle Morning to the task. Here are four steps you need to take to follow up your Miracle Morning with sustained focus.

1. Find Your Best Environment(s) for Unwavering Focus

Let's start here: *you need an environment that supports your commitment to unwavering focus.* It might be your spare bedroom, or it could be your backyard. No matter how modest, though, you need a place where you go to focus.

Part of the reason for this is simple logistics. If your materials are scattered from the trunk of your car to the kitchen counter, you can't be effective. A bigger reason, however, is that **having a place where you focus triggers the habit of focusing.** Sit at the same desk to do great work at the same time every day, and soon enough you'll find yourself slipping into the zone just by sitting down in that chair.

If you travel a lot, then your car, your suitcase, your hotel rooms, and possibly random coffee shops are part of your focus space too. Build habits for how you pack and work on the road, and you can trigger great focus the same way you do at the office. When you are prepared and always have with you exactly what you need, you can work anywhere.

2. Clear the Unfocused Clutter

Clutter is a focus killer, so getting rid of it is our next stop on the journey. There is a reason that Marie Kondo's book, *The Life-Changing Magic of Tidying Up*, is one of the bestselling non-fiction books of the last decade. Because decluttering both your physical and mental space will inspire a calm, motivated mindset.

There are two kinds of clutter, mental and physical, and we all have them both. We carry around thoughts in our minds like these: *My sister's birthday is coming up. I should get her a gift and card. I had a great time at dinner the other night. I need to send the host a thank-you note. I must answer the email from my new client before I leave the office today.*

Then there are the physical items we accumulate: stacks of paper, old magazines, sticky notes, clothes we never wear, the pile of junk in the garage, and all the trinkets, knick-knacks, and tokens that accumulate as we go through life.

Clutter creates the equivalent of a heavy fog, and to become focused, you need to be able to *see*. To clear your vision, you'll want to get those mental items out of your head and collected so you can relieve the stress of trying to remember them. And then you'll want to get those physical items out of your way too.

Here's a simple process to help you clear the fog and create the clarity you need to focus:

- **Create a master to-do list.** You probably have lots of things you haven't written down yet; start with those. Add the contents of all those sticky notes that clutter your desk, computer screen, planner, countertops, refrigerator (are there other places?). Put those notes and action items on your master list in one central location, whether that's a physical journal or a list on your phone so that you can clear your mental storage. Feeling better? Keep going; we're just getting started.

- **Purge your workspace.** Schedule a half (or full) day to go through every stack of paper, file folder stuffed with documents, and tray full of unopened mail—you get the gist. Throw out or shred what you don't need. Scan or file the ones that matter. Note in your journal any items that need your attention and cannot be delegated, then pick a time in your schedule to complete them.

- **Declutter your life.** Wherever possible, clean up and clear out every drawer, closet, cabinet, and trunk (including that of your vehicle) that doesn't give you a sense of calm and peace when you see it. This might take a few hours or a few days. Schedule a short time each day until everything is complete. Saying, "I just need a weekend to declutter," is a sure way to never start. Pick a single drawer and start there. You'll be surprised at how the little bursts of work accumulate. Try S.J. Scott and Barrie Davenport's book, *10-Minute Declutter: The Stress-Free Habit for Simplifying Your Home* for suggestions.

Getting physically and mentally organized will allow you to focus at a level you would never believe possible. It leaves your energy nowhere to go except to what *matters*.

3. Protect Yourself from Interruptions

In addition to our core business, we are writing this book together and have two children that we homeschool. As you can imagine, our time is critically important to us, just as we're sure yours is to you.

To avoid distractions and ensure that our attention is focused on the task at hand, our phone is almost always set on Do Not Disturb mode, which blocks all incoming calls, texts, or notifications like email and social media. This is a simple thing that dramatically increases our daily productivity and ability to remain focused on the task at hand. In fact, most phones will allow you to auto-set a Do Not Disturb mode for certain hours of the day, every day. We recommend returning phone calls and emails at pre-designated times, according to your schedule, not everybody else's.

You can apply the same philosophy and strategies to any notifications and/or alerts, time spent on social media, as well as your availability for colleagues, employees, and even clients. Do Not Disturb isn't just a setting on your phone. Let your team know when you're available and when they need to leave you undisturbed.

4. Build a Foundation for Unwavering Focus

Once you identify your focus place and begin the process of decluttering your life, you should experience a remarkable increase in focus simply from clearing the fog in your mind.

Now, it's time to take things to the next level. We use three questions to improve our focus:

- What's working that I/we should *keep doing* (or do more of)?

- What do I/we need to *start doing* to accelerate results?

- What do I /we need to *stop doing* immediately that's holding me/us back from going to the next level?

If you can answer those three questions and act on the answers, you'll discover a whole new level of productivity you probably didn't think was possible. Let's look at each question in detail.

What Do You Need to *Keep Doing* (or Do More of)?

Let's face it: not all tactics and strategies are created equal. Some work better than others. Some work for a while and then become less effective. Some even make things worse.

Right now, you're probably doing a lot of the right activities, and you'll be nodding right along as you read the coming chapters on growing and connecting as a couple. If you already know the things you're doing that are working, jot those down. Perhaps you're already using the Do Not Disturb function, or you're already well into a fitness challenge and feeling stronger each day, for example. Put that on the "what's working" list.

Make sure you're choosing things that increase your success. It's easy to keep the things you *like* doing, but you need to make sure that the activities you're doing are directly related to strengthening your relationship. Consider the 80/20 rule (originally the Pareto principle), which shows that roughly 80 percent of our results come from 20 percent of our efforts. Which 20 percent of your activities impact 80 percent of your results? It's easy to keep the things that you *like* doing, but this is reality—you need to make sure that the activities you're doing are directly related to your goals as a couple.

At the end of this chapter, you'll have an opportunity to capture in your journal the activities that are working. (Among them, we hope, will be that you've started doing the Life S.A.V.E.R.S.) Everything that's on that list is a "keep doing" until it's replaced by something even more effective.

For each of the "keep doing" activities on your list, make sure you're completely honest with yourself about *what you need to be doing more of* (in other words, what you're currently not doing enough of). If it's something you think you should be doing, but it's not moving you toward your important goals, it doesn't belong on your list. Perfection is not one of the goals here. Overworking yourself is ultimately unproductive and takes your focus off the important things.

Keep doing what's working and, depending on how much more you want to achieve, simply do *more* of what's working.

What Do You Need to *Start Doing*?

Once you've captured what's working and determined what you need to do more of, it's time to decide what else can accelerate your success.

We have a few top-shelf suggestions to prime the pump and get you started:

- Plan date nights

- Conduct weekly check-in meetings

- Schedule one overnight trip together this year

- Perform cleanup time every day

- Write what you're grateful for about each family member, especially your partner

- Create your *foundational schedule*—and coordinate that with the family calendar

- Be sure to get enough sleep, as outlined in the *Energy Engineering* chapter

- Schedule the housekeeper and get them on a rotation

We caution you to not become overwhelmed here. Keep in mind that Rome wasn't built in a day. You don't need to identify fifty-eight action items and implement them by tomorrow. The great thing about having a daily scribing practice as part of your Miracle Morning means you can capture everything. Then, one or two at a time, add them to your success toolbox until they become habits. Incremental improvements have a magical way of accumulating.

What Do You Need to *Stop Doing*?

By now, you've most likely added a few items to start doing. If you're wondering where the time is going to come from, this might be your favorite step of all. It's time to let go of the things you've been doing that don't serve you to make room for the ones that do.

I'm sure you do a number of daily activities you will be relieved to stop doing, thankful to delegate to someone else or grateful to release.

Why not stop:

- Eating unhealthy, energy-draining foods that suck the life and motivation out of you?

- Doing unnecessary household chores?

- Replying to texts and emails instantly?

- Answering the phone? (Let it go to voicemail and reply when the timing works best for you.)

- Reading/scrolling and posting on social media sites?

- Watching hours of television a day?

- Beating yourself up or worrying about what you can't change?

- Doing repetitive tasks such as paying the bills, buying groceries several times a week, or even cleaning your house?

Or, if you want to improve your focus dramatically in one simple step, try this easy fix: *stop responding to phone buzzes and notifications like a trained seal.*

Do you really need to be alerted the second you receive texts, emails, and social media notifications? Nope, didn't think so. Go into the settings of your phone, tablet, and computer and turn all your notifications OFF.

Technology exists for your benefit, and you can take control of it this very minute. How often you check your phone messages, texts, and email can and should be decided by *you*. Let's face it, most of us do not have jobs or lives that will result in a life-or-death situation if we do not respond immediately to a call, text, or email. We don't need to be accessible 24/7/365 except to our significant others and our children. An effective alternative is to schedule times during the day to check on what's happening, what needs your immediate attention, what items can be added to your schedule or master to-do list, and what can be deleted, ignored, or forgotten.

Final Thoughts on Unwavering Focus

Focus is like a muscle that you build over time. And, like a muscle, you need to show up and do the work to make it grow. Cut yourself some slack if you falter, but keep pushing forward. It will get easier. It might take you time to learn to focus, but every day that you try, you'll continue to get better at it. Ultimately, this is about *becoming* someone who focuses, which starts with seeing yourself as such. We recommend that you add a few lines to your affirmations about your commitment to unwavering focus and what you will do each day to develop it.

Most people would be shocked to discover just how little time they spend on truly important, relevant activities each day. Today, or in the next 24 hours, schedule 60 minutes to focus on completing the *single most important task you need to do*, and you'll be amazed not only by your productivity but also by how empowering it feels.

By now, you've added some pretty incredible action items and focus areas to your success arsenal. After you complete the steps below, head into the next section. There we will teach you additional activities to connect as a couple in the morning and how to combine them with the Life S.A.V.E.R.S. in ways you might not have heard or thought of before!

Putting Unwavering Focus into Action

Step One: Choose or create your ideal environment to support unwavering focus. If your focus is optimum when you're working in a public place, such as a coffee shop, schedule focused time-blocks at Starbucks®. If you work from home, make sure you've implemented step two, below.

Step Two: Clear your physical and mental clutter. Start by scheduling a half-day to clean up your workspace. Then, clear your mind with a brain dump. Unload all of those little to-do lists floating around in your head. Create a master to-do list, either on your computer, in your phone, or in your journal.

Step Three: Protect yourself from interruptions, both from yourself—by turning off tempting notifications—and from others, by putting your phone into Do Not Disturb mode and asking your circle of influence to leave you alone during your focused time-blocks.

Step Four: Start building your unwavering focus lists. Pull out your journal, or open a note on your phone or computer, and create the following three lists:

- What I need to keep doing (or do more of)?

- What I need to start doing?

- What I need to stop doing?

Begin jotting down everything that comes to mind. Review your lists, and determine which activities can be automated, outsourced, or delegated. Repeat this process until you are clear on what your process is and start time-blocking your days so that you're spending close to 80 percent of your time on tasks that produce results. Delegate the rest.

You've now got a great handle on how to incorporate the Life S.A.V.E.R.S. into your work and personal life. It's time to get into T.E.A.M., the morning routine you do *together*, and go deeper on the topic of the Legendary Relationship Elements of Partners, Friends, and Lovers. When you're ready, let's begin.

Tim and Jolie Cotten

Tim and Jolie Cotten are a couple that is madly in love. They are also quite unique; not in the sense of the marriage that they're in, but the support, encouragement, and hope they give to other families like them. While there are a lot of couples in the midst of the same challenges the two of them face each day, Tim and Jolie are rare in the way they put themselves out there for the world to see.

For both, this is their second marriage. Tim has 2 children from a previous marriage and Jolie has 3. They've figured out a recipe that makes co-parenting and being "step parents" work amidst creating a reflection and example of how to have a thriving relationship, not only to the children they are raising together but to other couples that may be struggling.

In 2016, they started The Blended Project (Instagram @the-blendedproject) to share their story. What started as a way to simply reflect on their journey and struggles together - a way to even remind themselves of it - has grown into quite a movement. They quickly discovered that other couples in their situation needed a guiding light of optimism, accountability, and love to navigate the complexity of being a blended family.

We had a chance to catch up with Tim and Jolie, where we had an honest conversation about their relationship and what has been the difference this time around.

[TC]: "I think there are 2 things that are very different this time around. 1 - We've learned how to have a 'mature love' that wasn't present before—at least not in my first marriage. 'Mature love' looks completely different. For example, it's reflecting on yourself— how *I* can be better—rather than blaming the other. It's about taking the initiative to fix yourself, instead of waiting for the other to do it first before you do. 2- It's about facing in the same direction when making decisions. In my previous marriage, we were always trying to 'convince' each other, facing opposite directions, which just didn't work. When we face the same direction, it makes it so much easier to grow and share the journey together. She still gets to be her, I still get to be me, but we are still moving *together*... no matter how fast or slow. This is so key."

[JC]: "We also over-communicate. This time around, there are a lot more moving parts, and having that constant communication is important. 'How are we going to raise the kids together, how are we going to co-parent with our 'ex's,' and how are we going to make our Faith an important part of our family?"

Tim and Jolie, through their own individual personal growth

journeys, recognized how vital this was to encourage and influence each other. On top of how self-awareness and emotional intelligence has impacted their marriage to each other, it also permeates into the harmonious system they have for co-parenting.

[TC]: "We've learned how to trade in short-term feelings for long-term goals, especially when it comes to the kids. I think a lot of other couples go wrong because they always try to 'stick it to the ex.' When you let go of trying to undermine them, it has a more positive impact on your marriage as well as the kids."

Focusing on the long-term goals and letting go of short-term feelings goes far beyond how they interact with their ex's. It's a profound statement of how we can all navigate our own relationships; whether they be with our intimate partners, our children, our extended family, and even our friends.

Tim and Jolie shared that this marriage to each other can be more challenging than their previous marriages, but it is so much more fulfilling. They face those challenges head-on, constantly communicate, and grow individually... which ultimately allows them to grow *together*, follow God's path, and let their relationship serve as a beacon of light for not only their children, but for any other couples out there that need hope, support, and encouragement.

SECTION III:
TOGETHER AS A T.E.A.M.

—7—
T.E.A.M.

"The strength of the team is each individual member.
The strength of each member is the team."

—PHIL JACKSON, six-time NBA championship coach

Behind every Fortune 500 company or Super Bowl title is a legendary *team*. Like a quarterback passing to the wide receiver for the winning touchdown, each teammate plays a specific, meaningful role.

As Andrew Carnegie once noted, teamwork "is the fuel that allows common people to attain uncommon results." We are looking for uncommon results if we want a legendary relationship.

Not all teams are created equal. Many, if not most, can't figure out how to work together and win. An overbearing team leader, a lack of direction, or a personality clash between teammates can stifle progress and bring your goal to a halt, leaving you with a mediocre team experiencing one loss after another.

As a pioneer in organizational behavior, J. Richard Hackman discovered that what matters most to team cohesion isn't behavioral; rather, "three enabling conditions"— (1) a robust structure, (2) a supportive atmosphere, and (3) compelling direction—must be met for teams to reach their full potential. These three conditions, coupled with a shared mindset, set the stage for a successful team. Other factors that enhance success include speaking and listening to each member equally, using energetic gestures when talking, collaborating for the good of everyone involved, and being proactive in discussions.

While the above description might make you think about joyous success in the workplace, the same concepts apply to the success of your partnership at home. The "robust structure" consists of the foundational beliefs, values, and visions couples create together. That "supportive atmosphere" is the condition in which the two people choose to encourage and uplift each other through the good and the bad times. And "compelling direction" involves looking toward the horizon of their vision and taking action on achieving the design for their relationship that they have created.

"We cannot accomplish all that we desire without working together."

—UNKNOWN

We were one of those unhappy couples many of us see too often. Our marriage was a big bowl of mediocre, just one of the majority of relationships that "suck." For many years, we were not teammates. Our relationship was sinking fast, and we were literally on opposing sides. Tit for tat, keeping score of who did what. Focused on blame. Living separate lives and never focusing on *us* and the limitless possibilities that our marriage could bring to the table.

Becoming a team seemed like an impossible task. We didn't listen to each other. We weren't connected. We were caught in the Partnership Loop, and we didn't know how to get out.

We absolutely sucked as a team for the first ten years of our marriage, though there were certainly moments of greatness tucked away here and there. There were periodic wins, but mostly just losses. What we lacked was consistency. We didn't have a playbook, we didn't have habits, we didn't track our success, and we certainly didn't pivot when things were not going well. Real challenges in our relationship were swept under the carpet. "These things are just too hard!" we thought.

Although you do need a lot of focus to develop the You Element to achieve your legendary relationship (and it's the foundational work that has to be done in order to bring your best self to the party), at the root of the problem is that most couples believe that their marriage should just exist and remain static (without putting the same level of energy they would give to create a legendary team or company). Sure, they might take a vacation once or twice a year or have a date together now and then (if they're lucky enough to plan it). But simply going through the motions doesn't create success, and certainly not legendary success.

Winning teams don't just go through the motions. Winning teams have a game plan. Winning teams have a strategy. Winning teams then execute on that strategy with unwavering focus.

Once we created a vision for what our level 10 relationship could look like and the plan to make it happen, we then made commitments and took massive action, trying anything and everything to gain momentum in that direction. We will share our process with you at the end of the book, in section 4.

While there were many strategies we created to reconnect us as a couple and to connect us as a team, one activity we developed stands out as being paramount to getting us back on track. It's been so important to us that we *still* practice it every single day after our own Miracle Morning practices.

T.E.A.M. for Couples

Creating a morning routine for our relationship was more of an accident than an intention, at least at first. Our individual Miracle Morning practice was sacred to each of us, but we were craving more time together without the kids to stay on track with the habits we had committed to. We were grappling with finding more time alone to talk about our marriage and about our family and discovering simple ways to connect with each other. So, we would wake up before our daughters did and combine our morning time together. Often, we would meditate together or listen to a visualization. Sometimes we would read our affirmations to each other. Nothing was off limits as we experimented with that morning time together doing our S.A.V.E.R.S. It was a nice, peaceful time to have coffee together and just share ourselves with one another. The beauty is that you, the reader, get the benefit of our experimentation with what worked the best and what mattered the most for our valuable time together.

We noticed during our morning time together, we would hold hands or even just touch knees. We also found ourselves simply talking about things we learned the day before, or sometimes a simple quote a friend had shared could spark a discussion. We remembered that expressing gratitude for each other during the tough times was critical to getting our relationship back on track, so this idea of appreciation for each other was a great way to start the day, too.

It was really just a fun time for the two of us to experiment with the best morning routine possible. We looked at the importance of the Four Legendary Relationship Elements: YOU, PARTNERS, FRIENDS, and LOVERS. How could we streamline this process so that these elements were represented? And because our calendars were so tight, how could we identify the *most* important things we could do for our marriage during this time together?

We decided that our own personal Miracle Morning routine, practicing the Life S.A.V.E.R.S., was something we wanted to do for ourselves. Since the You Element was the very first thing we had to rebuild to reconnect to each other, and because Hal's S.A.V.E.R.S. were so vital to that transformation, we would, of course, continue doing them.

Additionally, we feel strongly about growing together, and we have a lot of fun learning and sharing new information with each other. Spending a few minutes with each other and teaching the other about something interesting or cool we learned was a way to not only grow our individual You Elements but also combine each of our personal growth journeys into a collective learning experience where we intentionally grew together.

We also found that the morning was an ideal time for the two of us to run through the activities, goals, and events for the day just so there weren't any major surprises or things to be easily forgotten or lost in the shuffle. It was a great time to touch base and make sure our personal and family obligations were being met, and we were not "stepping on each other's toes." We want to be sure our Partners Element remains strong!

Like we mentioned before, expressing gratitude is a cornerstone of any connected relationship. If you read any relationship expert's advice, you'll see that sharing gratitude is almost always recommended. Plus, it's a great way to start the day with a loving appreciation for each other. Just like in an amazing friendship, it's never a bad idea to give your partner a verbal (or even physical) high five!

We also loved the idea of some form of physical touch in the routine. It felt so connecting to include that, whether it was holding hands or snuggling. It was a good way to create a spark, flirt, and grow in our Lovers Element.

Having these four extra practices added to our consistent morning routine made all the difference. We noticed that we could even get it done in 10 minutes if we wanted but were happy when we were gifted an hour by our daughters! The important part is that this was a small habit we did every day. From those small habits and rhythms, a ripple effect is created, building something magical that is even greater than the sum of its parts.

It just made perfect sense to us that at the heart of The Miracle Morning for Couples was INDIVIDUAL (You) growth and development and then TOGETHER (Partners, Friends, Lovers) growth and development. We would do our own S.A.V.E.R.S. by ourselves and then add these extra four practices together after that.

Each one of these became a vital component of our Miracle Morning together and a connected extension of our individual morning routine—essentially a Miracle Morning ... for Couples.

THE MIRACLE MORNING
for COUPLES

You
S.A.V.E.R.S.

You
S.A.V.E.R.S.

Together
T.E.A.M.

We called this additive routine T.E.A.M.

T - Touch | E - Education | A - Appreciation | M - Meeting

Being a great team is at the heart of any legendary relationship, and we experienced colossal results from spending this intentional time together in the morning. Because of this, it's become a formal part of our marriage plan.

The great thing about this morning routine is that it works for couples who may currently feel distant from each other as well as couples who feel that their relationship is strong since the activities not only promote connection when there is little but propel connection when there is already an abundance of it.

Let's take a closer look at each of the activities in T.E.A.M., the research and reasons behind their importance, and some ways you can implement them into your morning routine, your relationship, and your life.

T IS FOR TOUCH

"To touch can be to give life."

—MICHELANGELO, Italian sculptor,
painter, architect, and poet

One of our greatest needs is to be connected, especially to our significant other. While there are plenty of ways to help create this kind of connection, most are not as basic and so ingrained in our biology as simple, familiar touch. Additionally, one of the most common complaints in struggling marriages is the lack of physical touch and intimacy with a spouse. This is especially true if one or both partners come from a family that wasn't very affectionate or grew up with parents who weren't outwardly loving with each other.

Touch plays a crucial role in generating and enhancing love. People feel more satisfied in a relationship in which physical affection is a significant part of their routine. A legendary relationship needs connection and touch; without it, your marriage will slowly wither and die. If you can't be consistently intimate with your partner, whether physically, emotionally, or both, you cannot expect to have a lasting, successful relationship.

The Science of Touch

From the moment we are born, human touch is a vital component of healthy infant development.

Margaret Atwood said, "Touch comes before sight, before speech. It is the first language, and the last, and it always tells the truth."

Research shows that touch has direct and crucial effects on the growth of the body and the mind as well. The findings are inarguable. From birth to age five, physical touch plays a fundamental role in a person's development. We often think about the impact it has on the bond between parent and child. However, a wave of documented studies proves that there are incredible emotional and physical health benefits from touch. The research suggests that touch is key to human communication, bonding, and health, as well as healthy brain development, confidence, and social intelligence.

A review of research conducted by Tiffany Field, a leader in the field of touch, found that preterm newborns who received just three 15-minute sessions of touch therapy each day for 5-10 days gained 47 percent more weight than premature infants who'd received standard medical treatment.

"It is the first language we learn," said Dacher Keltner, a professor and researcher of psychology at the University of California at Berkeley. Touch remains, he said, "our richest means of emotional expression" throughout life.

His research helps us know that touch builds up collaborative relationships. Touch reinforces reciprocity between our primate relatives, who use grooming to build up cooperative Partnerships. Studies are showing that touch signals safety and trust. It soothes. Basic touch calms cardiovascular stress. It activates the body's vagus nerve, which is intimately involved with our compassionate response, and a simple touch can trigger the release of oxytocin, a.k.a. the "love hormone."

Touch reduces anxiety and stress, while increasing trust, intimacy, and connection.

The science of touch convincingly suggests that we're wired—we need—to connect with other people on a basic physical level. To deny that is to deprive ourselves of some of life's greatest joys and deepest comforts.

To bolster the idea of creating a legendary team, consider research that was conducted at UC Berkeley, led by psychologist Michael Kraus, to see how touch impacts all sorts of teams and their performance. They reviewed teams in the National Basketball Association, one of the most expressive arenas on earth, to note if there was any correlation between the number of touches between players and success in the win column. In his group's research paper, they noted that teams that were more touch-bonded (expressing more fist bumps, high fives, chest bumps, and hugs) were more successful than those that were not.

But what about our more intimate relationships? Could the same measure of touch correlate to success, say, in marriage? Is it possible that the simple daily habit of some form of physical touch, however small, be part of the recipe for creating a legendary team?

According to Laura Guerrero, coauthor of *Close Encounters: Communication in Relationships* and researcher of nonverbal and emotional communication at Arizona State University, "We feel more connected to someone if they touch us." Isn't this what we are aiming for? Connection?

And for marriage researchers and authors Dr. Charles and Dr. Elizabeth Schmitz, "To touch someone you love is to acknowledge their presence and to communicate your desire for them. That's why the most successfully married couples amongst us do it so often." They even noted that touch outranks sex in characteristics of a successful marriage. The Schmitz's believe it's "the accumulation of touching" and the reciprocity of touch that increases intimacy and relationship satisfaction.

If You Don't Feel Like Touching (or Starting Small)

When we almost divorced, the idea of any physical contact was foreign and flat-out uncomfortable for us. We would go weeks at a time without touching, and when we did touch, it was generally out of some feeling of obligation. When the conversation would come up about our lack of intimacy, we had a lot of tension, deep frustration, and embarrassment.

We understand that many couples reading this may not be in a place where they feel comfortable displaying this type of affection. And that's perfectly normal. There was a time when the two of us didn't hug, didn't hold hands, and didn't even want to be in each other's presence. So, we get it.

We had to take the pressure off intimacy, giving ourselves the permission and freedom to step back and work on ourselves and the other Relationship Elements before we felt like touching each other. We started with the You Element, got our Partnership in order, and learned to become Friends again. Once we began to respect and like each other, falling back in love, cultivating that Lovers Element was much easier. Through the process, we started to plant seeds of intimacy in small ways.

Although we were able to jump in with both feet and take massive action on our relationship plan, we understand the science of creating new habits and are huge proponents of starting small for most couples. You can't run a marathon without weeks and even months of shorter training runs. Every activity, especially if it's new or if it has been a while since you've practiced, takes patience and time.

Steven Guise, author of *Mini Habits: Smaller Habits, Bigger Results* says that when we're just getting started, we should make our habits "stupid small." Want to get better at push-ups? Do one push-up per day. Want to start a meditation practice? Then start with one minute per day! You can do those things. After a time, you might be doing 100 push-ups per day or meditating 30 minutes per day!

And so, when using touch in your Miracle Morning routine, you may need to break the ice by doing just that: starting "stupid small." These seemingly small gestures have benefits larger than they could seem. Not just in the given moment, but for the rest of the day, as well as for years to come when they are part of your daily routine. You are generating a large supply of mini positive moments with every little touch. That ratio of positive to negative moments just keeps growing and growing. You are adding small bits of connection with your partner every single day.

Touch was vital to helping us become more vulnerable with each other, especially in the bedroom. To this day, it's the Lovers Element that we must work on the hardest as the pinnacle of passion and true intimate connection. Because we know we can have easy slip-ups in this element, we make sure that the simple act of touch is placed within our Miracle Morning for Couples each and every day. In the Lovers section of this book, we'll give you some pointers that worked for us when we were improving this element and share what we do when we backslide.

Bring Touch into your Morning Routine

Touch comes in many forms. And the wonderful thing about its part in your morning routine is that it doesn't have to take up any additional time, as it can be done simultaneously with the other activities. If you're ready to bring touch into your morning routine, consider the following simple ideas to incorporate it:

1. A simple, low-pressure way to foster touch is to hold hands. While talking together, just hold hands on the couch!

2. Have contact with the knees. When we were just starting our combined morning routine, we would often meditate together, sitting with our legs crossed and one of our knees touching the other's knee.

3. Cuddle. If you're feeling more connected, it's easy to snuggle during your time together.

4. Stroking face or hair. This is a little more intimate, but it feels amazing and can even set a flirtatious tone for the rest of the day.

5. Sit together with your legs across your significant other's lap. This one has become the most common form of touch for us in our Miracle Morning together.

As you can see, these examples seem rather obvious. But it's the awareness of actually doing them that makes it count. By placing touch square into your morning routine together, you'll find that eventually, physical touch and even flirtation become commonplace in your relationship. The idea is that one day, you don't even have to think about doing it!

For those of you who are in a more physical and connected relationship already, you can take the advice of Ryan Michler, host of the podcast *Order of Man* and author of *Sovereignty: The Battle for the Hearts and Minds of Men*. Lance was telling him about our morning routine together and the inclusion of touch, and Ryan suggested that sex shouldn't be off the table. To which Lance replied, "Sure … I guess another thirty seconds in the routine wouldn't be a problem!"

But all joking aside, if the two of you are feeling that a more intimate experience can be included in your "touch time," by all means, go for it. Sometimes, when the time is right, we do, too! We'll continue to talk about ways you can customize your Miracle Morning for Couples activities to suit your needs, but this might be the best one yet!

Touch Throughout the Day

Here are some ways to introduce touch after your Miracle Morning or in the evening:

1. Hug when your significant other comes home. This can quickly incorporate a loving attitude and a "welcome" or "I miss you" vibe. It can also set the tone for the rest of the evening and mitigates the stress of the workday into your home life.

2. Foot rubs. This is a no-brainer. Who doesn't love foot rubs at the end of a long and stressful day? It also shows great support from one partner to the other.

3. Bury your head in their shoulder. If your partner is feeling especially stressed, this is a great way to express support and comfort.

4. Flirt. A light caress of the neck, pat on the butt, or whatever else your partner enjoys (be sure to know what that is!) can set up some exciting sexual energy, tension, or intimacy.

Final Thoughts on Touch

We often don't realize how infrequently we physically touch our partner. But, as with any other rhythm or habit, the more awareness you have of a challenge and the more often you take the necessary actions to overcome it, the more momentum is gained. When you apply those actions to your routine, so they're done subconsciously, you'll be more consistent in completing them.

Touch is important for sustaining a healthy relationship, but it's also necessary for our feelings of connection, safety, and overall well-being. People who experience regular loving touch benefit from increased oxytocin levels, which not only has been associated with lower heart rates and lower blood pressure but over time can decrease a person's risk for many serious health ailments. Scientific research tells us that effective touch is important for our emotional and physical well-being. Additionally, developing a rhythm of touch improves overall intimacy, cultivates your ability to be vulnerable with each other, and can vastly improve the Lovers Element of your relationship. The more you connect with your partner—with even the smallest physical gesture—the happier and healthier you'll both be.

E IS FOR EDUCATION

"Love does not consist in gazing at each other, but in looking outward together in the same direction."

—ANTOINE DE SAINT-EXUPÉRY, French writer and poet

Have you ever had that experience of leaving the movie theater with your significant other, chatting endlessly of all the highlights and lowlights of the film you just watched together? Sometimes you might even be especially chatty if the movie grabbed you in some special way that needs to be shared. The two of you may have even talked about it all the way home, or even continued that discussion as you got into bed. What you saw and what you appreciated together produced an intriguing dialogue that you didn't want to end.

Well, the Education portion of your T.E.A.M. time is kind of like that, except that—hopefully—it won't take up your entire morning routine … unless you'd like it to!

Grow Together, Not Apart

The education practice of your Miracle Morning routine together is where we create a connection between our own personal growth journeys. Doing this hosts a large spectrum of possibilities, no matter where each of you is in your own individual journeys. If one of you is still a little unsure about what topics interest you, then the other partner has the opportunity to guide the direction and kindle the fire. If both of you are already "full steam ahead," then this part of your T.E.A.M. just opens each other's worlds to so many new subjects to explore.

Whichever the case, shared learning can mitigate the chances of couples growing apart or in opposite directions. It specifically allows each of you to say, "This is what I'm learning about, or this is important to me, and let me share something interesting with you!"

It brings a part of your adventure of growing your You Element to the T.E.A.M. so you can experience those adventures together. It catalyzes the two of you to level each other up.

We also like this activity for The Miracle Morning for Couples practice because it works not only for couples who are just beginning this shared-learning journey by opening up a Pandora's box of conversation and communication but also for couples who are already into personal growth, by furthering and deepening their own development, cementing the information in their brains through teaching, and elevating the relationship through new interests and perspectives.

Master the Topics

There's also a little hidden benefit we noticed by adding education together in our morning routine.

Shared learning has the byproduct of topic mastery. When we read something, we retain very little of that knowledge unless we do other activities with that information. Many people underline books or write in the margins, which is a great start, but we can do even more.

The ultimate test of your understanding of a subject is by seeing how clearly you can convey it to another. And who better than your intimate partner? You can improve your presentation skills and organizational thought in a safe environment. And, even better, you can get fresh and even contrasting perspectives from the other person. This takes the learning to a whole new level as well.

The great thing about the education activity is that there are so many ways to do it. There are two basic ways we've incorporated this activity into our morning routine: (1) through shared learning and (2) by listening to or watching content together.

Below are just a few ideas that we've used. They can take as little as 3 minutes, but the average time we spend is about 15 minutes, mostly because we just really enjoy our time learning together. The great thing is that there aren't any rules. You can even spread a subject out over several mornings.

1. Share the things you read during your personal Miracle Morning (a.k.a. your S.A.V.E.R.S.). If you're getting a lot of great stuff from a book, share some of the new ideas or quotes you're seeing with your partner.

2. Watch a TED Talk together. Many times, we find a new TED Talk to watch, or even a talk or lecture one of us has watched before that we want the other to see. We try to keep them short so that we can talk about the best parts after we're finished.

3. Listen to a podcast together. Podcasts can be long, but we've broken them up into chunks when we don't have time to listen to them in one sitting.

4. Consider joining Brian Johnson's Optimize membership. Brian Johnson's content has meant so much to our relationship. We've been listening to his Philosopher's Notes for years and now often watch his daily, short, +1 video series. We

even watch them with our daughters all the time. Check it out at www.optimize.me; it's inexpensive and one of the highest-value memberships available!

5. Do a book club with each other. We've had a lot of fun reading books separately and then discussing the chapters together to share our own perspectives and insights with each other. In fact, we enjoy this activity so much that we've even created videos where we share with our community our own takeaways and relationship stories.

6. Get to know each other and strengthen your Friends Element! Who said the sharing had to be from another person's content? If one of the ultimate goals in your relationship is to know each other deeply, then why not use this time to do just that? When we were resurrecting our marriage, asking each other questions about our childhood, our values, our dreams—from the simple to the complex—had a profound impact on our growth together. There are many resources out there, like Table Topix and other question cards; even a simple Google search may point you to some great relationship questions you could ask each other. To get you started, here are some things we asked each other during that time:

a. What was your most embarrassing moment during your childhood?

b. If you could learn one new skill, what would it be?

c. What was your favorite summer activity as a kid?

d. What was the time in your life when you were the most nervous to do something?

e. If you could meet and have a conversation with anyone, living or dead, who would it be?

f. If you could go back in time, what is one piece of advice you would give your younger self?

g. What's the most spontaneous or craziest thing you've ever done?

h. What's the most fun you can remember having with one of your friends as a kid?

i. If you could have one superpower, what would it be and why?

j. What is the best meal you have ever eaten?

These questions may seem elementary, but the most important thing (especially if your communication with each other isn't strong right now) is that they ignite FUN and create a safe space that will spark deeper conversations down the road.

As we look back and think about it, both of us have learned so much from each other during the education portion of our T.E.A.M. time together. It's pretty astounding the conversations we've shared by simply "teaching" the other and the knowledge we've gained by watching, listening, or reading something together.

Final Thoughts on Education

At the end of the day, the education activity in the couple's morning routine enhances your communication with each other. It goes way beyond just the short amount of time you spend on this each morning and positively influences the way you interact with each other after you've commenced the rest of your day. The benefits are limitless. You can optimize your own personal growth through the mastery of a subject by teaching it to another, find conversation spark, share in your personal growth journey together, and improve your love connection through inspiring each other with new knowledge. It can also lead the two of you to establish new values from those subjects or ideas. It can even reveal to the two of you new horizons or frontiers to guide your family.

A IS FOR APPRECIATION

"At times, our own light goes out and is rekindled by a spark from another person. Each of us has cause to think with deep gratitude of those who have lighted the flame within us."

—ALBERT SCHWEITZER, theologian, writer, humanitarian, philosopher, and physician

"We can only be said to be alive in those moments when our hearts are conscious of our treasures."

—THORNTON WILDER, American playwright and novelist

The benefits of a gratitude practice are endless. Shifting your focus to the positive can dramatically change your happiness. Studies show that people who are consistently grateful are happier, more satisfied with their lives, and have a stronger immune system.

If you've already been practicing The Miracle Morning, chances are that you already practice some form of appreciation or gratitude. Your silence or meditation practice is a great place to feel into that pinnacle of thankfulness.

As children, we're taught to say "thank you" automatically in return for a favor or gift. We try to instill this virtue into our offspring,

even reminding them at very young ages the necessity of expressing thanks. On this surface level, we are taught that gratitude is an
appropriate social response. But, unfortunately, sometimes that's as
far as our level of appreciation goes; "thank you" tends roll off our
tongue subconsciously.

Appreciation is rooted in the Friends Element, and this practice
is a beautiful bridge to the Lovers Element. Appreciation is an expression of love that we too often don't use enough, which is why it
is included in our morning routine together.

So, how can we use true gratitude and thankfulness more fully to
cultivate healthy relationships?

Appreciation in Your Relationship

Too often we forget, or perhaps never really learned, the true and
magical value appreciation can have in our lives and especially in our
intimate relationships.

Way beyond just saying "thank you," gratitude is a spiritual way
of being. When we truly feel gratitude, we experience heartfelt awe
and appreciation for the goodness of something outside ourselves.
Having gratitude toward someone or something means respecting
its value and treasuring how unique, beautiful, or indispensable it is.

Unfortunately, unhappy couples have often stopped showing appreciation for each other. This appreciation deficit typically occurs
long before the couple becomes aware of the existence of marriage
problems or feelings of dissatisfaction. Sadly, as marriages move past
the honeymoon stage, couples go from appreciating and loving every
little detail about each other to taking each other for granted. Perhaps we get caught up in the stressful day-to-day details, but this lack
of appreciation for one another easily leads to disconnection.

Amie Gordon, a psychology research scientist at U.C. San Francisco, blames this for the downfall of many relationships: "You get used to having your partner in your life and forget why you chose to be with them." We become deadened to our spouse's special qualities and strengths and instead focus on things we perceive as weaknesses or traits that annoy us about them.

These slumps leave couples confused, discouraged, or even resentful. Maybe they feel their partner is no longer as great as they once thought. They wonder where that spark from when they first met went and begin yearning for what "was" instead of what "could be." It can be incredibly discouraging to not feel appreciated—you may even feel like your relationship is over. These feelings often leave couples wondering what to do next.

While there may be many different reasons why couples initially stop showing appreciation for one another when this pattern continues unchecked, significant marital problems and relationship troubles can result.

The Benefits of Appreciation

Mutual gratitude and appreciation can go a long way in healing many relationship problems. Expressing appreciation is a powerful first step in the efforts to regain that spark, to feel that love again. Daily reminders of genuine appreciation can deepen intimacy and make a healthy relationship even stronger. This isn't just an opinion, either; new studies support the idea that gratitude is an integral part of deeply connected relationships.

A study performed by Dr. Gordon explored the role of gratitude and appreciation in maintaining long and healthy relationships. In the study, 50 committed couples were given a week to fill out appreciation journals. On days when one partner reported feeling more appreciated, they tended to appreciate their partner more the next day.

Couples who had ongoing reciprocal appreciation were less likely to break up in the next nine months and even reported being more committed at the end of that time. The researchers concluded that a nourishing cycle of encouragement and appreciation provides extra incentive to maintain our relationships.

Appreciation can also effectively resolve conflict. All couples have disagreements and arguments. What distinguishes the marriages that last from those that don't is not how *often* they argue but *how* they argue and how they treat each other during those moments and ongoing every day. They lean into that conflict, seeking to understand each other instead of forcing their opinion or will upon them. These couples make it clear that they are listening to and digesting what their partner says, thereby showing that they value their partner's opinion. These acts of leaning in and seeking to understand come from appreciation that is felt and expressed, day in and day out.

In times of conflict, appreciative couples also use touch or some other form of physical encouragement, such as hand holding or an encouraging pat on the leg. Touch is already a big part of The Miracle Morning for Couples routine, so we hope you are beginning to see the additive benefits of developing these skills together.

All in all, when we appreciate our partners, we develop trust for and respect in them. When we feel appreciated, we feel needed and encouraged. We feel heard. We feel understood.

Some couples either are not naturally appreciative or have forgotten how to show appreciation. Just like the other activities the two of us commit to in our morning routine together, we were falling flat on this one when our marriage was at its lowest. We needed to take steps to share gratitude for each other.

Luckily, our behavior and thoughts are malleable; just as we fall out of patterns of love and gratitude, we can grow back into them. The key to sparking healthy relationships with gratitude is to take the initiative. Don't wait for your partner to be the first to make you feel good. Take matters into your own hands.

Learn to Appreciate, Together

Again, start with small and easily achievable goals. Here are a few simple exercises you can do, ideally during your morning routine together, but they can also be done any time of day:

1. <u>Focus on what's great.</u> Instead of thinking about what might not be going well in your relationship, focus on what aspects *are* going well. Write them down. Read the list back to yourself often. Then, share it with your partner.

2. <u>Create a small gratitude journal just for your partner.</u> This was something we did early in our attempt to rekindle our love for each other. During this activity, we would reflect on our partner and say what we were thankful for in them. This is especially helpful if one partner has been having some bad days. Expressing gratitude and then hearing it back from your most intimate partner can change your perspective rapidly, suddenly turning those terrible days into ones with love and meaning.

3. <u>Reminisce.</u> Recall why you married your spouse in the first place. What qualities or behaviors first attracted you to them? What do you value in them right now? In what ways has your relationship benefited you? What roadblocks have you overcome before? When a marriage is in strife, bad memories can consume your feelings about your partner. When you deliberately focus on the highlights of your life together, it helps you push out bad memories and nurture positive emotions about your union. This can be an incredibly powerful exercise that can have a lasting effect on strengthening your bond.

If these things still seem challenging, start small. Notice something simple that your partner does that you appreciate, and share that with them. The point is to *start*!

Appreciation is a skill that you cultivate; nurture it in yourself, and soon you will see positivity radiate back at you.

Words from a Former Apathetic Spouse: aka, Lance's Testimony on Appreciation

"Being thankful is not always experienced as a natural state of existence, we must work at it, akin to a type of strength training for the heart."

—LARISSA GOMEZ, actress and screenwriter

As someone who didn't practice gratitude regularly, showing appreciation was exceptionally challenging for me to get into the practice of. But over time, I've gotten so much better at it. In fact, I consider gratitude a virtue and one of our relationship's and family's core values.

I was never much of an empathetic person before, and I think this had something to do with my lack of appreciation not only for Brandy but regarding just about everything I should have been grateful for in the first place.

Perhaps my former apathy developed from my career as a critical care pharmacist; or perhaps it was from the sudden death of my mom in a car accident when I was twenty years old. I'm not exactly sure, but I had certainly developed some emotional calluses long before I was married and had kids. I would even justify my behavior as "stoic," but I was anything but.

In fact, my daughter came to me a few years ago and said, "Daddy, why don't you ever cry? I've never seen you do it."

This statement from her left me speechless. She was right. I hardly ever cried then.

The irony is that I've learned that Brandy's empathy is one of her biggest strengths and one of the things about her for which I now have the most gratitude. She has taught me how to feel into situations and, well, to be more appreciative of them.

Because of her, I've been able to tap into empathy, especially for couples (and specifically men) in distressed relationships. And from this empathy, appreciation has sprung.

Like many other people, the practice of gratitude has given me a brand-new perspective on life. It helps me to calm anxieties and fears. It helps my marriage to Brandy thrive. It allows me to grow more connected with my daughters.

And it may seem juvenile or silly to say so but expressing appreciation and being grateful—even for the smallest of things—makes me so much happier.

My best tool for gratitude, especially in drawing closer to Brandy, was a journal. Like Hal writes, make it part of the scribing you do during your personal Miracle Morning S.A.V.E.R.S., and then share what you wrote with your partner during your time together.

Even if it's not something about the relationship, share with them something else you're grateful for. Brandy did this for me a lot. She sees the world with appreciative eyes, and I get the benefit of those eyes helping me see the world in ways I never thought possible.

You have the power to give that same gift, too.

Final Thoughts on Appreciation

Genuine demonstrations of appreciation need to come from your heart. Sometimes couples (especially couples in distress) need to work hard to find something they feel appreciative about—and they end up getting stuck in a problem-focused process.

Don't let this stop you. Work toward expressing gratitude even for the smallest things your spouse/partner does. Small demonstrations of appreciation have a powerful cumulative effect.

When couples work toward creating a shared rhythm of gratitude, their relationship brims with positivity, and cycles of positive interactions feed the emotional bond that connects the two of you.

Cultivating these genuine expressions of appreciation can be hard. Be patient. It will take some practice to see the benefits, especially if there has been ongoing tension in your marriage or relationship. However, with persistence, and by adding this aspect to your morning routine, ongoing appreciation will help you gain positive momentum between the two of you. After all, we all want to feel appreciated by the most important other in our life.

M IS FOR MEETING

*"If you do not change direction, you may end up where
you are heading."*

—LAO TZU, Chinese philosopher and writer

We once heard that when a rocket is fired toward space, it is off its target for over 90 percent of its journey. It continuously makes corrections when needed to eventually get to where it needs to land. The same should be true with your life and your relationship. The two of you will continually need to communicate about your vision, making corrections along the way for what might not be working or serving your relationship.

The meeting practice of your Miracle Morning together helps keep the more complex elements of your relationship on track: your Partnership.

Legendary companies have meetings, and so do legendary couples. They check in to see how things are going and adjust where necessary. They discuss the plan and schedule for the days and weeks ahead. They consistently and proactively move their lives forward by bringing awareness to what is working and what is not. We know this sounds simple, but it is a grossly lacked step in relationships.

Regular check-ins and meetings are crucial to the success of your relationship, and your mornings may not be enough time to get through all the things while you are first getting started. A weekly meeting is very important, too. Just as companies often have a Monday morning meeting, couples should do the same. For example, our family has a Sunday evening meeting to go over the goals and calendar for the week. This part of your Miracle Morning practice is designed to set the schedule for the rest of that day to keep you on track and help you gain rapid momentum in the success of your relationship.

The Benefits of Meeting

According to a study by the American Management Association, effective meetings can accomplish many things for a company, but it's obvious that the benefits for companies are the same benefits for intimate relationships.

Meetings keep you moving in the right direction

Problems and issues are a part of life, and they will certainly be part of your relationship. Unfortunately, little issues become big problems when they are not proactively addressed. Over time, resentment builds. One partner is harboring frustration while the other is unknowingly continuing the behavior that caused the frustration. Proactively and respectfully addressing issues helps us to properly pivot and avoid repeating the problem. This is especially helpful as we are working toward a new direction as a couple by designing a legendary relationship. There are a lot of moving parts, and being proactive about discussing or addressing what isn't working is one of the most important steps.

It is equally as important to know what *is* working. Not only do we all want to know that what we are doing is making a difference, especially when we are working toward something so important, but we also want to do what's already working with confidence. This is when we begin to feel hopeful, and the momentum builds. When you find something that works well to move you closer to where you want to be … do more of that!

Either way, consider this a quick trial-and-error check-in and take the pressure off. Know that you will try things that don't pan out, and some things will feel like hitting the jackpot. You will get to your goals faster if you don't take the feedback personally and just move on. When something isn't working, modify your actions or stop doing them, and when something is working, continue what you're currently doing or do more of it!

Your time and effort are well spent with meetings

Even when couples are making efforts to connect more, often they might be doing the wrong things and spinning their wheels. Whether it be the expression of love or even the way we try to repair disagreements (e.g., our way of apologizing), we often act in the way we believe would make ourselves feel better. Unfortunately, it's often wrong for our partner. For example, when we would have disagreements and arguments in the past, Lance would try to hug Brandy as an attempt to repair the problem. But Brandy often wanted anything *but* being hugged in those moments. What made her feel better (being left alone to process) was not at all what made Lance feel better (hugging). Once we began to have these meetings consistently, we opened the floodgates of honesty and got our marriage moving in the right direction.

If we want success, we don't have time to do the wrong things for too long. We want to know when we are doing the right things at the right time. The only way to know this is to check in and confirm. Decisions are made faster, and we become more confident, efficient, and honest in our communication.

Additionally, we want to make sure our calendars are in sync. Nothing is more frustrating when you and your partner are not on the same page because the events for the week or day were not communicated, coordinated, or put on the schedule. Conflicts and time-wasting can be avoided when you continually check in

Meetings help momentum build faster

In Darren Hardy's legendary book, *The Compound Effect*, he describes the simplicity of incremental steps. Darren illustrated this with the story of the magic penny.

In this story, you're faced with two choices: you'll get $3 million in cash today, or you'll get a penny today and double the amount every day for thirty-one days. Which would you prefer? Let's say you take the $3 million now and your friend opts for the doubling penny. If you take that $3 million today, you look pretty smart on day one when your friend only gets a penny. You still look pretty smart on day five when your friend gets sixteen cents. And on day ten when he gets $5.12. You're still on top. Your friend may be questioning their decision. Twenty days later, your friend is only up to $5,243. This is when the magic of the compound effect kicks in. Fast forward to day thirty-one, and your friend has gotten $10,737,418.24 to your $3 million.

As Darren says, "Very few things are as amazingly impressive as the 'magic' of compounding pennies. Amazingly, this 'force' is equally powerful in every area of your life."

Just like we've talked about before, the magic of your legendary relationship is built on the compound effect of small habits (pennies) that add up to monumental connection (wealth) for the two of you.

How to Have an Exceptional Miracle Morning Meeting

There are several things that the two of you can do to have successful morning meetings together. While we tend to oscillate between the following topics, the progression of our morning meeting time together has included the following subjects:

Status of our marriage:

Nearly all our early check-ins revolved around how we were doing as a couple. Our commitment to continued honesty and breaking through the fear of discussing how we were doing as a couple dominated these meetings. Additionally, to break free of any passive-aggressive behaviors (notably by Lance) or aggressions (notably by Brandy), we made a commitment to address challenges or triggers immediately so that we could practice ways to discuss and resolve them quickly. It can be hard to receive what could be negative feedback from your partner, which is what makes the act of appreciation a great counter-weight to heavy conversations. But trust us, being 100 percent honest with each other will move you faster to creating the most vulnerable and connected relationship possible, with both of you becoming artfully skilled in conflict resolution and overall communication.

These meetings were also the stage where we began a more intentional practice of active listening: a way for us to master the art of understanding each other, shifting perspective, and cultivating grace and compassion.

While any reasonable Google search can tell you the characteristics of active listening (be attentive, avoid judgment, ask open-ended questions, summarize, etc.), it's important to highlight that great listeners have more connected relationships. According to psychologist Carl Rogers, active listening is at the heart of every healthy relationship. It's also the most effective way to bring about growth and change. Those who are heard tend to be more open, more democratic in their ways, and often less defensive. Good listeners refrain from making judgments and provide a safe environment and container for speakers.

By listening carefully when someone speaks, we're telling them we care about what they're saying.

Like we've mentioned, challenges will happen, and disagreements will be part of your relationship. The morning meeting gives the two of you the opportunity to tackle any issues head-on, first-thing, so that the rest of your day can be spent taking a positive turn to resolution and forward momentum.

Schedule:

While this may seem like a no-brainer, going through your schedule for the day (and maybe even the next couple of days) means more to the relationship than you might think. This is where the wheels of the Partnership system take motion. When we don't get our calendars in sync, disaster can strike. Some of our earliest and most contentious arguments (shouting matches, really) in our marriage revolved around one of us forgetting to carry out some sort of task or commitment. And until we consistently checked in with each other's personal commitments and coordinated the ones that involved our family, nothing could derail us more. The morning meeting can also help create decisions for the day (such as what to have for dinner, who is taking care of what obligations, etc.) so that we aren't left scrambling later in the day to get those things done. Having the day-to-day tasks co-organized consistently opens the doors and affords the two of you the time to work on your Friends and Lovers Elements of your legendary relationship.

To be best equipped and ready to go over our calendars and commitments together, we make sure we have the following:

Planners/Journals: We use the same planner (one that Brandy co-created). Our planner not only has our schedule, but it also has a space for tracking personal habits and commitments (to each other and to ourselves) that we can then also talk about during our morning meeting. While everyone has their own preferences on planners, we have found it helpful to use a similar system so that we are managing on a similar format/platform. This is also a great tool to have in order to go over any relationship status issues you've written down or journaled/reflected about during your S.A.V.E.R.S. time.

Electronic calendars: Lance is much more "electronic" than Brandy when it comes to tracking his calendar. He needs to have reminders for nearly everywhere he needs to be, along with the most important habits and commitments. He still uses his planner, but having the reminders pop up on his phone is helpful for his forgetful (or easily distracted) brain. Therefore, during our morning meetings and check-ins, any time-based appointments are placed on each other's electronic calendars. These include trash day, deadlines, appointments, and especially those items pertaining to our daughters (e.g., school pick-ups/drop-offs, soccer games, play dates, birthday parties, etc.).

Pat and April Flynn

We had the privilege of interviewing Pat Flynn, best-selling author and host of the *Smart Passive Income Podcast,* about his relationship with his wife, April.

Pat told us that, "a thriving and healthy relationship is one that involves a lot of communication. Communicate early and communicate often. We've noticed that a lot of friction happens when there is a lack of communication."

Pat and April have a daily rhythm where meeting with each other is a high priority. They check in each morning to set the tone and schedule for the day.

These daily meetings "are key, and we find that when April and I are in a very healthy state of mind, our kids are happier. It creates the aura in the family, and it starts with April and me." Their morning meeting helps them to prioritize their marriage and their family more than anything.

Continual, daily check-ins allow Pat and April to also make long-term goals for their family and their relationship. It allows them to make very intentional decisions and conscious choices. It keeps them in sync. It helps them to know what each of them needs from the other.

"For an entrepreneur who has a lot of things on his plate; to allow April to understand what my needs are, and me understanding where her needs are... the earlier we understand that, the more likely we are to be on the same page."

For Pat and April, consistent communication does more than just keep their schedules in check.

"It's everyday thinking to myself how lucky I am, how truly grateful I am for the support and love that I get from her. It is knowing that I have a partner in raising two human beings... to try and make them amazing citizens who can contribute in this world. It is going to bed every night next to her and just thanking God for the amazing life that He's given me and the partner that I have. It's understanding that there's comfort in knowing, with her, no matter what happens we're going to be there for each other. It motivates me to go bigger and try different things knowing that she's going to be there for me. But also knowing that if I get a little "too big", she'll let me know. I think we complement each other really well in that way. I also can uplift her and give her thoughts and ideas in the life that she didn't even imagine was possible. We've worked hard for this. Nothing is perfect. But we've made it as perfect as can be by communicating often, by being visionaries together, and by understanding what our priorities are and making sure that we know how to bend, but not break. I am blessed and so thankful for her."

Final Thoughts on Meeting

Your morning meeting is the setting for cultivating and growing your communication skills together. If things aren't clicking right away, don't get discouraged, especially if having these types of check-ins are new for the two of you. Remember to have grace. Remind each other that developing any skill takes loads of practice and repetition. Celebrate that you both are trying to create a legendary relationship and that these moments are part of those small habits that create the compound effect of your Partnership. Stay committed to the process. Just keep at it, and over time the two of you will become pros.

Customizing Your Miracle Morning for Couples

While the formats of your S.A.V.E.R.S. and T.E.A.M. time have been laid out for you in this book if you feel the need to make some changes here and there, go for it!

While we stick to the order of things you've read most of the time, we experiment and do things differently from time to time. It's fun, and it freshens things up.

For example, we've even done some of the S.A.V.E.R.S. together, like guided meditations or visualizations, affirmations (co-creating them for our family or marriage), and exercise. This can be beneficial when we've wanted to spend more time together or even be more efficient.

Also, depending on any time constraints you may have on certain days, touch can be done while you're engaged in the education, appreciation, and meeting parts of your morning routine so that it doesn't take any extra time if you don't want it to. However, as we mentioned earlier, touch can mean a much more intimate experience for you if your relationship is at a place for it.

Every couple's schedule is different, so be sure to experiment and find what works best for you. We've noted that we can feel victorious if we take 15 minutes to engage in our T.E.A.M. activities. But we cannot stress how important the Life S.A.V.E.R.S. are; when schedules are busier (life has its ebbs and flows!), we've pushed T.E.A.M. activities to other times of the day, like before bed. This is perfectly fine! If the two of you take five to thirty minutes of intentional and focused time together each day, you are winning and well on your way to creating a legendary relationship!

In the next section, we're going to dive further into Legendary Relationship Elements of Partners, Friends, and Lovers. But like the S.A.V.E.R.S., we would encourage you to get started with T.E.A.M. so that the two of you can build a rhythm together for your morning routine. The next section should certainly inspire more stuff to discuss and share during your T.E.A.M. time, but having that habit in place will make it a lot easier down the road.

— 8 —
TOGETHER PRINCIPLE #1:
PARTNERS

"We cannot accomplish all that we need to do without working together."

—BILL RICHARDSON, American politician, author, and diplomat

Partnership is the business side of your relationship. It is the environment you create together and for your family. It is making money, budgeting, saving, planning for the future, and all other financial aspects of life. Partnership is the daily running of your lives: chores, laundry, cooking, shuttling kids, and all the rest. It is the values, goals, dreams, and alignment of your relationship "compass" pointing in the same direction.

Partnership is the engine that runs the automobile. Without a great Partnership, you cannot move forward. Don't expect to experience the connection and joy of your Friendship and deep intimacy as Lovers when this element isn't working. This is where couples often feel most frustrated, irritable and stuck in their relationship. They get caught in the partnership loop without knowing how to get out.

Partnership has the most moving parts of any Element and takes the most skill to navigate. Take all the logistic components and add in the fact that you are 2 different people, from 2 different backgrounds, with different strengths and weaknesses. Some people may have had the benefit of learning how to navigate this Element as a kid by watching someone—like their parent(s)—do it successfully. However, it is safe to say that most of us didn't learn effective Partnership before we got together. We haven't met a couple who both came from model parents, and clearly it isn't taught in school. So, start this section with grace for yourselves. This is a complicated area, and most of us don't know what the heck we are doing. For the most part, we're just trying to survive.

It is no surprise that this area is where most of our arguments happened. "You didn't do this, I always do that, this didn't get done at all, and I can't believe we forgot to…" We were overwhelmed with the mile-long to-do list and packed calendar (you know, kept in our heads and hardly ever written down) and felt like there was never enough time to get it done. We were such a mess, and there wasn't enough time; we were inefficient, with no direction. All of this combined into the perfect storm, creating major resentment toward each other.

This is why it is so important to continue working on You in the process. The emotional awareness and your personal growth will have a positive impact on how the two of you navigate through the choppy waters of Partnership.

WHY PARTNERSHIP MATTERS

"It takes both sides to build a bridge."

—FREDRIK NAEL, writer and blogger

If the engine of your automobile isn't running properly, you aren't going anywhere. If the alignment is off, then you go in different directions. You need to be able to lock arms and agree on the vision of your relationship and the vision for your family for your Partnership to thrive.

The Partners Element of your relationship is where the real teamwork takes place. Great teams have a common goal of winning, while each player understands that they have a specific role in the game and must work together to reach the championship. Each player practices their gifted skills or strengths, honing them for the big game. That's when teammates come together, each with his or her own sets of skills and strengths, working as a team to win. In football, the quarterback can't be upset with the wide receiver for not being a good thrower, and the wide receiver doesn't get upset with the quarterback for not being the best catcher. They've agreed to their roles and strengths.

The same can be said for relationships. Each of you has roles, and each of you has strengths. Additionally, when you learn to celebrate those strengths in each other, instead of focusing on each other's weaknesses, we can begin to set a plan in place to craft an amazing Partnership. You and your spouse can then share in the goals you have established, and from there the possibilities are endless.

WHAT A LEGENDARY PARTNERSHIP LOOKS LIKE

"Attraction is common. What is rare is having someone who wants to grow and build with you, a soul partner, a soul confident, a soul mate."

—BILLY CHAPATA, writer, author, and creative

When you're in a legendary Partnership, you are a well-oiled machine. You feel the security of your relationship foundation forming and begin to feel safe knowing that the two of you have your life handled together. Respect and admiration naturally form because you trust each other on a deep level. Trust in each other is the backbone of the Partnership. You know you are in this life together, and your partner has your back no matter what.

Consider a Navy SEAL team: without trust, that team will fail. Most people think others are crazy to consider entering a smoke-filled room full of bad guys with guns who want to shoot them. But SEALs do it with gusto because they trust their teammates. And because of that trust, the attack can proceed. They can't do their jobs—say, clearing the right side of the room—unless they can trust that the teammate coming in right behind them will do their job and clear the left side of the room. They trust and rely on each other.

But it takes a tremendous amount of discipline for the first SEAL not to look to the left when they are clearing the right side of the space like they are supposed to do. But that's the beauty—and the benefit—of trust. With trust comes success.

When the pressures and not-so-great events of life happen, which they do in all relationships, you know that together you've got it. This is because you have a solid partner with whom you can get through anything. You don't blame your partner, especially for the roles or strengths that they aren't supposed to have. You love and celebrate where they do excel, and you trust each other to get the work done.

You begin to create a life that matters to the two of you without the influence of the rest of the world because you have confidence individually and together.

The momentum and buildup begin, and you begin to feel excited to have fun and enjoy each other again.

CREATING A LEGENDARY PARTNERSHIP

"Coming together is the beginning. Keeping together is progress. Working together is success."

—HENRY FORD, American captain of industry
and business magnate

To become a success in this area, we studied successful people, companies, and teams. What do they do to achieve legendary results? Why are some people happier than others? Why do some companies go under and some become an "Amazon"? Why do some teams barely make the playoffs and others consistently win championships?

Remember, every legendary element starts with You. Winning teams have winning players, they have ringers, and they have people who took their natural talent, trained like no one else, and put in the work to become the best at their specific role. They have coaches who have had prior success and guide them to take the right steps. They create a plan and outline those steps to make that plan happen, and then they train like they have already won!

The following are six principles that can help the two of you grow and develop your Partners Element. We will guide you with a few questions for each one that you can use in the final section of the book.

FIVE PARTNERS PRINCIPLES:

1. CORE Values

2. Roles

3. Finances

4. Parenting

5. Home/Schedules

PARTNERS PRINCIPLE 1: CORE VALUES

> *"It's not hard to make decisions
> when you know what your values are."*

—ROY O. DISNEY, American businessman
and co-founder of Walt Disney Productions

> *"Your Core Values are deeply held beliefs that
> authentically describe your soul."*

—JOHN MAXWELL, American author,
speaker, and pastor

People experience greater fulfillment when they live in alignment with their values. Core values are those we consider most important in our lives. They are part of us. They highlight what we stand for and are literally what we value in life.

We all have core values. But, sadly, most people are either not clear about what their core values are, or they know but don't live in alignment with them. We often don't understand what's most important to us. Instead, we focus on the values of our society, culture, and media. Without identifying and aligning with your core values, you may stumble through life feeling directionless, conforming to someone else's life, getting stuck in bad habits, and frequently spend-ing quality time on things that take time away from true fulfillment and happiness.

In Mike Merriam's book, *Closer Than You Think*, he says, "Your core values are the heart of your positive core and should inform every decision you make." Values should guide our behavior, assist us in making clear and confident decisions, and provide us with our personal code of conduct. According to Lifehack.org, some of the benefits of having your core values are that you:

Make Better Decisions—When you come across the need to make a decision, your values can help you make the right call. Some-times emotions get in the way of good decision-making, but stop-ping to ask yourself what someone who values X would do in this situation just might help you come to a more clear-headed, less emo-tionally affected decision.

React Better—Values can help ensure you behave in a way that matches who you want to be at your core. People often react quickly in situations, especially difficult ones, and they don't always take the time to think about what they are doing before they do it. You can use your values to reflect on situations as well, to help you decide, for example, if you need to apologize for something. What a helpful little tool!

Avoid Distractions—Legendary couples need time for each oth-er. Knowing your core values helps you spend less time on things that just don't matter and allows you to move closer to your goals more quickly. Identifying your values will help you rule out the things you really do not want, need, or believe are important. People are con-sumed with so much these days. Weed the time- and energy-wasting distractions out of your life!

Increase Your Confidence—Identifying your values increases your level of confidence because it brings about a sense of stability and safety to your life. When you know what you want, it doesn't matter what other people want. When you know what is important to you, it doesn't matter what is important to other people. This will naturally bring a sense of confidence to your life.

Increase Your Happiness—You've developed a purpose, reacted better in difficult situations, made good decisions, developed opinions, and increased your confidence. It's fair to say you might just feel a little happier!

Developing Your Core Values

Getting clear on your core values is the first step to developing the foundation of your Partnership.

When you connect with your personal values, you can start to chart a course that's right for you. And when you honor your personal core values consistently, you experience fulfillment. Here's how to develop your core values:

- Start with Google! Search "list of core values" and find one that has 100 or more core values listed.

- Ask yourself, "What do I stand for? What do I value?"

- Circle the ones that resonate with you the most. We find it helpful to start a timer and give yourself 5-10 minutes for this exercise.

- Narrow your circled choices down to 5 or 10 Core Values.

- Now it's time to get clear on why each one is important to you and connect with what that means for you and your relationship together. You can also pick a quote that resonates with you to represent your Core Values.

Here is an example of one of our Core Values:

COURAGE

*"Everything you've ever wanted
is on the other side of fear."*

—GEORGE ADDAIR, humanitarian

Importance: Uncertainty and fear hold us back; we need courage to move forward and act anyway.

Courage = Fear + Action

This Means: We do hard and uncomfortable things because our goal is always more important than our fear in the moment.

PARTNERS PRINCIPLE 2: ROLES

*"What will happen if we think about what is right with
people rather than fixating on what's wrong with them."*

—DONALD CLIFTON, American psychologist and developer of
StrengthsFinder, an online psychological assessment

There is a lot of responsibility in sharing a life with someone. We go from taking care of everything ourselves and doing it our way to sharing our life with someone else, sharing where we live, our finances, and major decisions for our future.

Most of the time, these assignments happen with little to no forethought. This can work if you get lucky or have 2 strong people with high emotional intelligence and personal awareness. Sometimes the assignments don't happen at all. In both scenarios, most people end up either frustrated or with things falling through the cracks. We call this the Partnership Loop. It's an endless cycle of putting out fires due to a lack of planning and direction.

If we consider what makes a successful business partnership work, each partner comes with specific strengths and experiences. One may be good with finances and cash flow, so they take the role of CFO. The other partner may be great at vision and growth strategy, so they serve as the CEO. In times of frustration, the CFO doesn't say to the CEO, "I can't believe you didn't make more money this week." And the CEO doesn't ask the CFO why the bills aren't paid, or the budget wasn't forecasted properly. Why? Because they have evaluated, who is best for what position, assigned the roles, and moved forward with the commitment of those roles.

Same goes for sports teams. Some football players are better suited for throwing, some running and some blocking. In baseball, you have players devoted to hitting, throwing, or catching.

Legendary teams and companies know the importance of roles and strengths, and when done right they win and/or teach others to do the same.

Guilt and frustration are what we experience when we feel like we should both be doing the same things—or *all* the things—in our relationship Partnership. "I always do this, you never do that." Well, duh. My role is this, and your role is that. This simple yet powerful adjustment in thinking changed everything for us. Think about it: if a company wants to be successful, they remove such redundancies. Same goes with couples.

Getting this right was important to us fully developing our Partnership. Heck, getting this right caused us to fight a whole lot less ... at least on simple things (or so they seem to us now). Brandy is a passionate, creative, scattered dreamer, with brilliant ideas and so much confidence that she will try things that sometimes fail. Lance is grounded, highly intelligent, and slow and steady; he gets things done right the first time. Instead of getting frustrated about what the other isn't good at, we can celebrate and leverage each other's strengths

We all have strengths, and we need to play to them.

There's an internet meme that says, "Everybody is a genius. But if you judge a fish by its ability to climb a tree, it will live its whole life believing that it is stupid." Obviously, climbing trees isn't the fish's strength. And here's the kicker: if it is continually asked to keep trying to climb a tree, it might lose its ability to do what it was meant to do: swim! Not only is the fish spending time on something it isn't as good at, but it is losing its natural talent. We see this with couples everywhere (and with kids as well, but that's a topic for another day).

One partner may be great at going out and making money, and the other partner has guilt that they don't do the same. And the one who is at work feels guilty for not cleaning the house or helping with the kids' schedules.

This guilt and resentment come up out of a pure lack of defining roles and looking at your relationship as a Partnership.

You need a strong offense *and* defense to win the Super Bowl. You need both a salesperson and a finance person to have a successful business. Yet in our relationships, we feel guilty for not playing the other's position or, even worse, we make our partner feel guilty for not playing our position.

At the end of the day, you two have you two. So, you can either lift each other up for what you are good at and own your talents, or you can get stuck pointing fingers and feeling guilty.

Key Questions:

What am I good at?

What do I enjoy?

What is my partner good at?

What does my partner enjoy?

PARTNERS PRINCIPLE 3: FINANCES

> *"Money is a tool. Used properly it makes something beautiful; used wrong, it makes a mess."*
>
> —BRADLEY VINSON, certified financial education instructor, author, coach, and speaker

Let's get something straight: we are not money experts. There are plenty of books out there that can help you with this subject if you want to create more money. In fact, Hal co-wrote a book with David Osborn for this series that's called *Miracle Morning Millionaires* and is amazing. Additionally, we're not going to give you advice on how to manage your money.

But we know that money matters are the cause of more fights among couples than children, chores, and work … possibly combined. Money issues create anxiety and stress, which, in turn, can wreak tons of havoc on your relationship. In fact, money is one of the top reasons for divorce.

What we have done well, regardless of how much money we have in the bank, is to create a plan, budget, and communicate about our finances. We are completely and 100 percent transparent about where we are financially. There aren't any secrets, and there aren't any surprises. This is the key!

Whether they're about unexpected expenses or insufficient savings, how a couple manages money squabbles is a strong predictor of that couple's stability.

Despite all the conflict couples have over money, 55 percent of couples do not set aside time on a regular basis to talk about financial issues.

It helps to have a good understanding of our own, and then of our partner's, mindset around money. Understanding and communication are what is going to create a great Partnership around finances.

What is your money style? Are you a saver or a spender? It helps to know this information about each other and be open about it.

How are your budget skills? Do you even have a budget? Have you created one but don't follow it? How satisfied are you right now with your budget? One of you is probably better at handling the budget than the other. That's OK. This a Partnership, after all.

One aspect of your money mindset that is vital is each of your financial fears. In most relationships, each of you has some sort of fear, even if you're financially stable or thriving; we all harbor fears. Perhaps you feel you don't have any influence over your family's finances—that you don't have a say. Maybe you have fear around financial security, that there's not enough to live on or for emergencies. You might not feel respected by your partner regarding finances. You might have a fear that you won't be able to realize your dreams, that you might not be able to do what you want in the future because of money.

Regardless of your financial fears, talking about them is what is important. With some honest and kind communication, you can find ways to soothe each other's fears and anxiety over money so that you can create a plan for the future.

While it's not fun to talk about, debt is critical for couples to discuss if they want to improve their Partnership on money. The vast majority of couples have debt, whether it's a mortgage, car loans, credit cards, school loans, or something else. How comfortable are you about your current debt situation?

Key Questions:

What are our expenses?

What are our financial goals (such as freedom)?

What does our debt situation look like?

What steps can we take to reduce our debt?

How much income do we have?

How much income do we need?

Who will make what money?

Who will handle bills and budget?

How often will we meet to review our finances?

PARTNERS PRINCIPLE 4: PARENTING

"Having a 2-year-old is like owning a blender you don't have a top for."

—JERRY SEINFELD, American stand-up comedian and actor

Hands down, becoming parents was the single most life-changing event for us. We will never understand how hospitals are able to send first-time parents home with a new baby without a manual. Especially a manual that tells us what to do to stay together or at the very least not want to strangle each other.

We felt like we went into a vortex. Looking back, we had no idea what we were doing. We found ourselves in counseling after our first daughter was two years old. This helped us stay married, but it really didn't provide us any direction. We basically treated some symptoms, but we didn't get to the root of the syndrome. Then we had daughter number two, and we were completely disconnected and nearly separated by the time she was two years old.

The reality was, before having kids, we didn't have a plan. We got married, had kids, and figured it will all work out. It did for our neighbors, cousins, and definitely people on TV. We were good people: intelligent, kind and successful.

So what was the problem?

Raising good kids into great adults while staying in love and connected as a couple takes work. Real work! It takes having conversations about how you will do the hard things and enjoying the moments that go so fast. Like anything, it takes having a plan, making commitments, and taking intentional action.

Our parenting style probably differs from just about anyone else's … and everyone else's does as well. No set of parents is like the next. So, once again, we don't want to give you parenting advice in this book. As he did with finances, our friend Hal co-wrote *The Miracle Morning for Parents and Families* with Mike and Lindsay McCarthy that has a ton of great advice. It even has a routine for kids called C.H.A.R.M.S. that's wonderful.

What we do know is that the two of you need to get on the same page. Sound familiar? You guessed it. Your parenting requires tremendous communication and planning.

If you have children, ask yourself the following questions.

Key Questions:

What values do we want to instill in our kids?

How will we help them develop these values?

What is our discipline method?

Who handles specific logistics? (Like homework, getting them to practice, or who is going to do all the yelling when they misbehave . . . joking! Just making sure you're still with us.)

What type of education do we want them to have?

PARTNERS PRINCIPLE 5: HOME/SCHEDULES

"Your home should tell the story of who you are, and be a collection of what you love. "

—NATE BERKUS, American interior designer, author, and television personality

"The bad news is time flies. The good news is you're the pilot."

—MICHAEL ALTSHULER, author, speaker, and coach

We come from different homes and have different ideas of how a home should be kept, how it should feel, what matters and what doesn't.

ENERGY: Brandy loves interior design. Every house we have lived in has felt homey. However, she can be a mess. She moves fast and leaves a tornado behind her. Lance doesn't have an opinion about the decor, but he sure cares if the house is cluttered and messy.

Lance is good at consistently picking up, staying on track. He's the perpetual cleaner. Although messier than Lance, Brandy is an excellent binge cleaner and organizer. When the house is out of control, she hits the RESET button well! When the house is out of control, Lance doesn't even know where to begin.

When we began to think about the energy we wanted in our home, descriptions came up like peaceful, welcoming, intentional. We had to find a balance that incorporated Brandy's desire for aesthetics and Lance's minimalistic tendencies. Although our home leans toward Brandy's decorative desires, it is much simpler, more peaceful, and has an intentional flow.

SYSTEMS: Before we had kids, our home life was simple. We didn't have a need for systems the way we do now. However, during the struggle years of our relationship, some basic home systems could have gone a long way. Now, systems are everything in our home. Some examples:

- Grocery/supply inventory and needs list (we keep ours on the fridge, although we hear Amazon's Alexa is a big help!)

- Chore and maintenance lists (daily, weekly, monthly, and yearly)

- Routines for us and the kids (morning, evening, and Sunday prep)

- Menu—what we're going to have for dinner each night that week and a list of the available items for each of us to make ourselves breakfast and lunch

LEVERAGE: Time is the most valuable asset we have.

When we were both working full-time (or more), we had a lot of help. Our support included a gardener, pool service, pest service, cleaners, laundry, help with the kids, and someone who came in a couple of times a week to do laundry, help pick up the house, and get us back on track.

Our lifestyle was extreme. However, even now, with much less busy schedules, having a house cleaner gives us back four hours each week to add value to a priority—spending time together or with friends, doing something that brings us joy or helps with our health or growth, or simply sitting and relaxing.

ROLES: We talk a lot about this because it is important. Remember, this is the Partnership section and, well . . . you are partners. Here is a simple way to separate out who does what:

First, make a list of everything that needs to be done and how often.

Now, take anything you enjoy doing. Then decide what you can leverage out. Next, take anything left that you are good at or comes easy for you (Brandy creates the systems, Lance never forgets to take out the trash). You are left with the stuff that no one wants to do. The only logical solution at this point is a game of roshambo (aka, "rock-paper-scissors") to divide them up.

SCHEDULE: A mentor of ours once said, "I can tell everything I need to know about someone by looking at their calendar and bank account." Time is our most valuable asset, and it takes time to make money. How you spend your time and money is everything. We were a complete mess in this area. If you looked at our calendars as a pie chart, you would have seen the majority of our time and effort going to making money and the other large portion to spending it. Our time together was virtually nonexistent, and the kids got our rushed leftovers.

Gary Keller, the founder of Keller Williams Realty and co-author of the bestselling book, *The One Thing*, has a brilliant, yet simple, system to help with this:

Get a year-at-a-glance calendar. Schedule in your priorities. Make time for your health, time for each other, time for your career, and so on. When you take a bird's-eye view of the entire year, you see how much time there really is. We all have the same number of hours in the day; it's how well we use them that makes all the difference.

Key Questions:

What energy do we want in our home, and how can we create this?

Where can we add systems for efficiency and maintenance?

What can we leverage (or hire out) to make more time for our priorities?

Who is responsible for what?

What system will we use for scheduling?

How often will we meet (every morning—duh!)?

Are we making sure our priorities are given ample time?

— 9 —
TOGETHER PRINCIPLE #2:
Friends

"Happy marriages are based on a deep friendship."

—JOHN GOTTMAN, Ph.D., marriage researcher
and clinician

Friendship is just that: you are friends! It is the part where you inspire, encourage, and uplift each other. Friendship is being in a mutual fan club. It is where the fun, joy, and deep connection take place. Friendship is laughter, thoughtfulness, and play. It is where you confide in each other and offer a shoulder to cry on. Friendship is where you have each other's back.

You got into this relationship because at some point you really liked each other. You enjoyed spending time together. You made each other laugh and made each other feel better when one of you felt down. The importance of having a solid Friendship in marriage is obvious; you need to feel great about simply being around each other, just like you do with your best friend or favorite buddy.

The goal is to enjoy each other's company. To know each other deeply, be playful, have good conversations, and find ways to be thoughtful and have fun with each other.

Friends bring joy, relaxation, support, and companionship into your life. You take time to get to know each other, and the more you know each other, the closer you are. Think of the difference between an acquaintance and a dear friend whom you have known for years. With the latter, your conversations flow easier, and you don't skip a beat. You know stories about their life and can talk about anything. You seek out common interests, and you do things together, like attending concerts, having dinner together, grabbing coffee, or maybe taking a hike. You know you have differences, and you respect and appreciate what they enjoy even though you might not enjoy it. Because when your friend cares about something, you care about it, too. You may even join them for activities that aren't your favorite just to see them smile. You talk about everything—the good, the bad, and the ugly. You share similar values and respect each other.

You know what's going on in their life and what they are struggling with. You know their deepest desires, goals, and dreams. And let's face it: one of the best feelings in the world is to be truly known.

Friends check on each other if something important is coming up to ask, "Hey, how do you feel about this?" If they experienced something, "How did it go?" Friends are supportive. "How can I help?"

WHY FRIENDSHIP MATTERS

"A friend is someone who picks you up when you are down and if they can't, they lay down beside you and listen."

—WINNIE THE POOH, fictional teddy bear

Great friends help you grow. Because they know your desires, goals, and values, they can be great accountability partners who call you on your BS and challenge you to be better. True friends are not only honest but willing to say the difficult thing if they know it is the right thing. Of course, we might hate it when friends give us tough love, but to become our best selves, we need supportive and honest people in our lives. We don't always agree with our friends either, but we choose to debate in a respectful and healthy way.

And so it is with the Friends Element of our intimate relationship.

The benefits of creating a legendary Friendship are endless. It can:

- Improve your mood. Spending time with a happy and positive partner can elevate your mood and boost your outlook.

- Help you reach your goals. Whether you're trying to get fit, give up smoking, or otherwise improve your life, encouragement from your significant other can really boost your willpower and increase your chances of success.

- Reduce your stress and depression. A healthy Friendship can boost your immune system and help reduce isolation, a major contributing factor for depression.

- Support you through tough times. Even if it's just having

someone to share your problems with, friends can help you cope with serious illness, the loss of a job or loved one, the breakup of a relationship, or any other challenges in life.

- Sustain you as you age. Retirement, illness, and the death of loved ones can often leave you isolated. Having people you can turn to for company and support can provide purpose as you age and be a buffer against depression, disability, hardship, and loss.

- Boost your self-worth. Friendship is a two-way street, and the "give" side of the give-and-take contributes to your own sense of self-worth. Being there for your friends makes you feel needed and adds purpose to your life.

Friendships are one of life's greatest joys in life and make us happier healthier and make us better people. So, who better to have a Friendship with than your partner in life!

So, let's talk about how to develop a great Friendship!

FOUR FRIENDS PRINCIPLES

1. Deep Knowing
2. Quality Time
3. Fun
4. Presence

FRIENDS PRINCIPLE 1: DEEP KNOWING

> *"To know another, and to be known by another - that is everything."*
>
> —FLORIDA SCOTT-MAXWELL, playwright, author
> and psychologist

To be truly known is one of the most special human experiences. Consider the comfort of an old friend or your most coveted family member. The foundation of your relationship is built on deep knowing. They understand you, even when your mask is off. They love and accept you, flaws and all. You get to be you, just you, and that is enough.

Experiencing this with your partner is how you begin the journey of deep intimacy. Consider when you click with a friend, and you want to deepen the relationship; the more you get to know each other, the closer you feel. You begin to feel comfort when you are around them—a sense of ease. How does this happen? Just like it did when we were kids: "Tell me about you, what do you like, where did you come from, what have you gone through?" These questions open the window to someone's soul.

It's sad to think that once most couples cross the threshold into a serious relationship, marriage, and having kids, the process slows way down. It's sad because, well, this is when it can get really, really good. This is where two people truly become soul mates.

You know them, and they know you. Your dreams, your fears, your past hurts. Let's be honest: it's scary. It takes vulnerability, and to do that, you have to create a safe place for each other. A place where the past is in the past, and there is no shame. A place where we are free to dream as big as we want and feel encouraged. When we decide to go deep with a Friendship, we want to know more about them, we encourage and inspire them, and we work hard to relate and even console them when they are sharing something "real."

What if we did the same for our mate? I want to know you: your life, your pain, your desires and dreams, the things that scare you and the ones that light you up. What might happen then?

This scary yet simple step changes everything. Small mess-ups are treated as exactly that because you know where they stem from and why your partner struggles. You both become more confident and adventurous intimately.

A simple place to start is by asking questions. While we were rebuilding our relationship, we would spend a couple of evenings a week sitting on our deck and pulling questions out of a hat. You can Google "questions to get to know your spouse," use TableTopics®, or throw in things that you want to know about each other. We also gave some suggestions in the education section of T.E.A.M.!

We recommend reading Gary Chapman's bestselling book, *The Five Love Languages*. It's one of the most important and referred books out there on relationship connection. These love languages (Words of Affirmation, Quality Time, Physical Touch, Receiving Gifts, and Acts of Service) give you insight into what means the most to you and your partner.

FRIENDS PRINCIPLE 2: QUALITY TIME

"Time is the currency of relationships. If you want to invest in your relationships, start by investing your time. "

—DAVE WILLS, pastor, writer, podcaster, and blogger

Gary Chapman's *The Five Love Languages* website says that, in the vernacular of quality time, nothing says, "I love you," like full, undivided attention. Being there for this type of person is critical, but *really* being there—with the TV off, fork and knife down, and all chores and tasks on standby—makes your significant other feel truly special and loved. Distractions, postponed dates, or the failure to listen can be especially hurtful. Quality time also means sharing quality conversation and quality activities.

Time is a precious commodity. We all have multiple demands on our time, yet each of us has the exact same hours in a day. We can make the most of those hours by committing some of them to improving our relationship.

The fact is that legendary Friendships take time, and legendary friends generously give time to their relationship. We live in a time when, if someone is off social media for an extended period, we feel disconnected from their lives. Reality is, we can do the same with the person living in our home because we are giving time to everything else. Are we so busy that we really don't have time? Or … are we spending the time we do have doing other things? We all know the answer. Every one of us has 24 hours in a day; it's what we choose to do with those hours that creates the quality of our lives. If you want a better relationship, give it more time.

When this topic comes up, we often hear similar excuses: "We are so busy," or "We don't have time to have a regular date night, go get coffee, stay up after the kids go to bed, or wake up early together." To be honest, those couples are simply *choosing* not to give the time.

Your relationship will be the sum of the time and effort you put into it. Period.

In the last chapter, we will dive into making time for busy people, but for now, just know it needs to be on your radar. There is no success if you don't invest time.

FRIENDS PRINCIPLE 3: FUN

"You don't stop having fun when you get old.
You get old when you stop having fun."

—RITU GHATOUREY, writer

Fun should be a top priority. It shouldn't be relegated to the bottom drawer, the one you open only when all the real work is done.

Psychology Today magazine states, "Play is serious business. This sounds paradoxical, and it is, inasmuch as something that comes so naturally to large-brained mammals, that fun is so vital. Play is a banquet for the brain, a smorgasbord for the senses, providing nourishment for body and spirit: sad then that as a society we seem to be starving ourselves of it."

Having fun helps you de-stress and forget your problems, worries, and responsibilities, even if it is for a couple of hours. Psychological aspect aside and biologically speaking, when you have fun, your body releases anti-stress hormones which enables you to relax, especially if you are taking part in activities that require physical energy. You can strengthen not only your mind but your body as well.

Partners who do things together become more closely connected and come to enjoy each other's company. That's because shared experiences give them something in common, and that helps make them feel good about each other. Couples who have established a habit of doing things together actually come to enjoy these activities more than those they do on their own or with other people.

FRIENDS PRINCIPLE 4: PRESENCE

"You don't build a bond without being present."

—JAMES EARL JONES, American actor

"Pay attention!" If you have kids, I'm sure you've passionately said this a few times. What causes them to lose attention? Most of the time, it's a distraction. The TV, a smartphone, video games … the wired world has distracted us from human presence. But it's not only children who aren't paying attention. Many couples allow distraction to slowly erode at the connection between them.

If you're having challenges with being present, eliminate the distractions. Turn the phone off completely, or put it away in a place you don't see it (we've known people to lock it in a safe!).

Additionally, we hope that the activities of T.E.A.M. will create opportunities for the two of you to practice presence, helping you to become experts at attentiveness with each other.

From time to time, our minds wander. That's normal. But when our partner is trying to engage with us, it's important to stop what we're doing, regain focus, and listen.

These attempts to engage with us are what Dr. John Gottman refers to as bids. They are calls for attention. They are a form of reaching out. A bid is any attempt from one partner to another for attention, affirmation, affection, or any other positive connection. Bids show up in simple ways—a smile or wink—and more complex ways, like a request for advice or help. In general, women make more bids than men, but in the healthiest relationships, both partners are comfortable making all kinds of bids.

Gottman calls the response to these bids—a way to establish the presence we're talking about—as "turning toward."

Why? Because in these crucial, yet seemingly small moments, you have a choice. You can either strengthen your relationship by turning toward your partner or slowly erode your connection with the continuous action of "turning away."

Bids can get tricky, however, and admittedly Lance sometimes missed more bids than he didn't, especially if they were based on negative emotion. "Turning toward" when a bid is wrapped in anger required Lance to have more self-awareness. Indeed, many men struggle in this regard, so it's important to pay attention. Bids usually have a secondary layer — the true meaning behind the words. Call it the difference between text and subtext. Turning away doesn't always mean a lack of response but can also be exhibited in defensiveness or malice.

Here's an example:

"Are we out of apples? I forgot to check when I was in the kitchen earlier." Partner A asks.

Partner B shrugs and doesn't look up from their smartphone (turning away).

Or …

Partner B puts the smartphone down and responds, "Hmm, I have no idea. But I'll check on my way out and, if we are out, stop into the store on my way back from the gym later and grab some" (turning toward).

The difference is that you intentionally take the time to tune in, actively listen to, and respond to your partner in a way that leaves them acknowledged and heard.

Another example:

Partner A: "You always just sit on your butt after dinner. Has it ever crossed your mind to help with the dishes?"

Partner B grows defensive and says, "Well, when do you ever take out the garbage?" (turning away).

Or …

Partner B says, "Oh, you're right. I am so sorry. I'll be better about helping after dinner" (turning toward).

Although this bid was cloaked in frustration, it was a plea for help. Being attentive, staying present, and turning toward in these instances, instead of hearing criticism and reacting defensively, begins a compound effect of positivity and will probably soften the response for future plea bids.

FIVE WAYS TO STRENGTHEN YOUR FRIENDSHIP

Long-term vitality and connection are maintained through moments of intentional Friendship woven throughout the course of your relationship. Here are a few ways you can create those moments:

1. Make small moments into pivotal experiences.

Think about the honeymoon phase of your relationship, that time when everything about your partner seemed fascinating. Emotions had taken hold of you, and everything from your partner's hair follicles to their crazy comments to the passionate way they looked at you drew you even closer to them. You were head over heels!

Fast forward a year or two into your relationship. No doubt there are moments that still draw you to your partner, but you notice that "flame" is a little less vibrant, and it seems like more of a chore to make time to be together.

This is when the intentional work of maintaining your marital Friendship is most important.

Couples in long-term relationships must learn to make the seemingly small and mundane moments pivotal occasions that show your partner you are in tune with their world.

2. Express genuine interest in your partner.

Do you do fun things together during your free time? You don't have to have the same interests as your partner, but you can absolutely enjoy time spent together by engaging in one of their (or your) interests.

Open yourself up to the opportunity of doing things you may not otherwise do on your own, for the sake of your relationship. What you will find is that, through your willingness to do so, these activities actually become enjoyable. The goal is not to force yourself to like golf if you don't enjoy golfing but to look for moments to share with your partner while you are golfing with them.

3. Make everything—even the mundane—an opportunity to connect.

As contrary as it may sound, the smallest ways that you acknowledge your partner's questions and expressions are the most significant in strengthening and securing your physical bond.

Daily experiences like doing dishes, folding laundry, watching TV, or cooking together can be opportunities for a deeper connection. These can be moments to share about your day, talk about your goals, or simply check in on how each other is feeling. When you practice your T.E.A.M. together in your morning routine, you set up the potential to carry out these connections during everyday activities.

What are some daily activities or rituals that you wish your partner would do with you? Would it be nice to have them fold laundry by your side (we actually do have "laundry-put-away parties" in our house), or simply sit together at dinner and have a conversation instead of silently scrolling through your phones?

4. Make your Friendship unconditional.

When you think of your closest friends, you probably know that there are few things (if any) that could dissolve the bond between you. There is an acceptance of your differences, an understanding that you may disagree on certain issues but love each other nonetheless.

Simply bringing this mentality into your relationship will do wonders for your connection and romance. Recognizing that you will have differences in opinion and ways of addressing certain issues that come up throughout your life can allow you to explore your partner differently.

Work stress, issues with the kids, challenges with other family members, and so many other things can overflow into your relationship. There should be no conditions when it comes to showing up for your partner. Treat them with the same understanding and unconditional support as you would hope to receive from them.

5. <u>Be on your partner's side.</u>

This goes beyond being able to accept your differences. When it comes to you and your partner versus the world, you should always take the side of your spouse. Show genuine interest in being on your partner's side, and never do or say things that could leave them feeling insignificant or alone. Stand up for your partner when you see them feeling uncomfortable in a social setting. Ground yourselves in your relationship by reminding your partner of your future goals when they doubt themselves.

As with any friendship, the Friendship between the two of you is a bond that must be nurtured and prioritized. Creating meaningful experiences, showing genuine interest in one another, prioritizing romance, and being on the same team are all simple, daily actions you can make right now to strengthen your connection. Cultivating these will become a lifeline for your relationship and, later down the road, could potentially save each other from otherwise drifting apart.

— 10 —
TOGETHER PRINCIPLE 3:
LOVERS

*"If you want intimacy in your marriage,
you must share life."*

—GARY CHAPMAN, author, and pastor

The Lovers Element involves true intimacy, deep love, kissing, sex, vulnerability, tenderness, and passion. Lovers is the aspect that no one else knows about each other except the two of you. For Lovers to thrive—to really be maximized—the other three Elements need to be that solid foundation you have been reading about. If You, Partners, and Friends are not strong, Lovers can feel nonexistent, superficial, or not truly connected. Legendary lovers understand their partner's desires and give to them selflessly. They understand the flowing dynamic of masculinity and femininity, especially in the bedroom.

When we get caught in the Partnership Loop, it is difficult to have consistent and thriving intimacy. When this area gets rusty, it can be awkward and emotional to address. This is why it is so important to develop your Friendship to feel comfortable and safe enough to allow the vulnerability necessary for this element to thrive.

When we put time and care into this area, we experience the deepest bond and level of intimacy we can have with another person.

Four Lovers Principles:

1. Flirting

2. Vulnerability

3. Energy (masculine/feminine)

4. Sex

LOVERS PRINCIPLE 1: FLIRTING

"Don't ever stop dating your wife and don't ever stop flirting with your husband."

—UNKNOWN

For whatever reason, once we are comfortably in love, we don't think we need to do the things we did when we were dating. Flirting when we first meet is what brings us together, and it is just as important in keeping us together. If we want to experience the feelings we had when we fell in love, we have to do the things that made that happen. If we want to keep the spark alive, we have to fuel it. Flirting keeps the flame going and sparks more frequent intimacy.

Flirting has myriad benefits for your intimate connection. It creates an opportunity to be playful, it's an ego booster for you both, and it helps keeps the flames fanned. It's a positive way to communicate your love to each other, a reminder that you still find each other attractive, and a technique for your children (if you have them) to notice your love for one another.

While the activities around flirting may still seem obvious, somehow along the way, we may have forgotten how to do it. So, just in case you're a little rusty, here are some ways you can flirt with your partner:

- Make it spontaneous. Don't flirt at the same time every day, especially right before bed. The fire is more effectively kindled earlier.

- Look into your spouse's eyes. You should make eye contact when flirting.

- Coy behaviors—a suggestive glance, a wink, a sexy smile, a pat on your spouse's rear, lowering your eyes, an arched eyebrow—all say you are still interested in your partner.

- Practice flirtatious physical touch, like a squeeze of your partner's hand or knee, a light touch on your mate's shoulder or back, or giving a long embrace.

- Don't forget about using a flirtatious tone of voice, leaning toward your spouse when giving a compliment, or placing a light kiss on your partner's neck.

LOVERS PRINCIPLE 2: VULNERABILITY

> *"Staying vulnerable is a risk we have to take if we want connection."*

—DR. BRENÉ BROWN, research professor, author, and speaker

Opening up to our partner can make us feel vulnerable and exposed, but it is the most important ingredient of a trusting, intimate relationship. One of the biggest challenges that couples face is being vulnerable with a romantic partner. After all, with over 40 percent of adults having grown up in a divorced family, healthy examples of intimacy may have been in short supply. In other cases, many of us were raised in homes where showing vulnerability was seen as a weakness. This is often true for the beliefs of men. Many women have more openness to cultivating and showing vulnerability with their mate but bridging the gap can be challenging.

What drives our fear of being vulnerable? Dr. Brené Brown says that vulnerability is often viewed as a weakness, but it's actually a strength. In her *New York Times* bestselling book *Daring Greatly*, she explains that vulnerability is the core of all emotions and feelings. She writes, "To feel is to be vulnerable. To believe that vulnerability is a weakness is to believe that feeling is a weakness. To foreclose on our emotional life out of fear that the costs will be too high is to walk away from the very thing that gives purpose and meaning to living."

Dr. Brown defines vulnerability as emotional exposure, uncertainty, and risk. With this definition, the act of loving someone and allowing them to love you may be the ultimate risk. Love is uncertain. It's risky because there are no guarantees. In fact, exposing your true feelings may mean that you are at a greater risk of being criticized or hurt.

However, vulnerability just might be the glue that holds a relationship together. It can help you navigate day-to-day life with a partner and allow you to feel comfortable letting your hair down with them at the end of the day. Likewise, it may be the lack of emotional maturity that comes from not showing vulnerability that can lead many couples down the path to divorce. If you are afraid of showing weakness or exposing yourself to your partner, you might not be aware that your fear is preventing you from being totally engaged in the relationship. You might be freezing out the opportunity to love deeply because you are afraid to let your authentic self shine and to share your innermost thoughts, feelings, and wishes.

Three Steps to Allowing Yourself to Be Vulnerable with Your Partner

While all relationships present risks, they are risks worth taking. Legendary relationships are within reach if you let go of fear and believe you are worthy of love and all the gifts it has to offer. Here are the three steps to allowing vulnerability:

- Visualize yourself in an honest and open-hearted relationship, and work toward allowing yourself to be more vulnerable and open with your partner. Communicate that this is something you are trying to do.

- Challenge your beliefs and self-defeating thoughts about accepting nurturing from your partner and showing compassion toward them.

- Don't let your fear of rejection or past hurts stop you from achieving the love and intimacy you deserve. Practice being vulnerable, rocking the boat in small steps so you can build confidence in being more emotionally accessible to your partner.

Intimacy can be an important source of comfort and provide predictability in an uncertain world. It is possible to be vulnerable and close to others without losing parts of yourself. By doing this, you'll be able to restore your faith in love, trust, and intimacy.

LOVERS PRINCIPLE 3: ENERGY (MASCULINE/FEMININE)

"I think of masculine and feminine energy like two sides

to a battery. There is a plus side and a
minus side, and in order to make something turn on,
you need to have the opposites touching.
It is the same in relationships."

—TRACY MCMILLAN, American author, television writer and
relationship expert

Masculine and feminine energy in a relationship is a formidably large topic. We could probably write an entire book on this matter (maybe we will one day!). But in this section of the Lovers Element, we want to be specific about how these energies play out (and therefore need to be understood) for the deepest part of your intimate relationship.

Men and women alike both exhibit masculine and feminine qualities. Each individual is different, and the balance of these energies will vary greatly. Brandy expresses masculine qualities quite a bit, especially as it pertains to her roles and drive in business. This energy got in the way at home when she brought it into her marriage to Lance.

It wasn't until she learned to balance her masculine and feminine energies that we were able to cultivate vulnerability and true intimacy, especially in the bedroom. Additionally, Lance needed to rebalance his energies to create a safer place for Brandy to feel vulnerable enough to let go and let her inner feminine energy shine. This was more easily accomplished through the thriving and loving Friendship the two of us had created with each other.

Traits that are most often associated with the feminine are things like connection, empathy, nurturing, and emoting. The feminine "she" is pure energy, flowing and changing like the water of a river and giving the banks of the river meaning and purpose. She has a diffused awareness, thinking many things at once, and she finds details and intricacies that escape the masculine. She is born to receive. She is most identified with her feelings and craves love deeply to feel fulfilled.

Drive, focus, assertiveness, and confidence tend to be seen as more masculine traits that set one up for success in business and the corporate world. Masculine energy is full of consciousness and is solid like a river bank, giving the flow of the river the freedom and safety to do what it does best. Thoughts are focused on goals, the future, security, and protection. The masculine is most identified with his purpose and productivity in the world, and he loves fulfilling a mission.

When it comes to sexual intimacy, it is important to identify those differences and seek to generate harmony between the two of you to have the most connection. We must create polarity.

In his book, *The Way of the Superior Man*, David Deida informs us that, "Sexual attraction is based on sexual polarity, which is the force of passion that arcs between masculine and feminine poles. All-natural forces flow between two poles. The north and south poles of the earth create a force of magnetism. The positive and negative poles of your electrical outlet or car battery create an electrical flow. In the same way, masculine and feminine poles between people create the flow of sexual feeling. This is sexual polarity."

LOVERS PRINCIPLE 4: SEX

"Once you have uncovered the secrets of mastering your sexual energy, you will feel a peace that you may have never known."

—ROBERTO HOGUE, relationship coach and author

It goes without saying that most couples want to improve their sex life. Being sexual is one of the healthiest things a couple can do.

Not only is a physical connection with someone good for your emotional and physical health, but it can also be wonderfully pleasurable. People who have active, regular sex lives in their intimate relationships tend to be happier, enjoy better physical health, and live longer than their celibate counterparts. When couples have happy, healthy sex lives—defined by having sex at least twice per month—they report being happier overall and dealing with the ongoing stresses of life better.

So, building on the idea of having harmony between masculine and feminine energies in your Lovers Element, how can we take action to experience the greatest fulfillment with our intimate partner for the relationship we have designed for each other?

While we are writing in generalizations here, there are some differences between men and women we need to highlight so that the two of you—with your growing Friendship, vulnerability, and trust—can begin an open conversation, especially if you both are currently dissatisfied with your sex life. The challenge is that there is a lot of miscommunication between couples, or lack of any discussion at all when it comes to emotional differences and needs in the bedroom.

In general, most men tend to focus on the physical aspects of a relationship. They are stimulated, drawn, and captivated by the sight of their mate. They get excited or at least interested quickly by visual or physical stimulation. Most men can be ready for physical intimacy in minutes. Once a sexual release is in the forefront of his mind, it becomes dominant in his focus. Men at this point are ready to move ahead with the process of seeking sexual release through intercourse.

Generally, men put a much higher priority on sex than women do, and women have a different orientation that demands a different approach. A woman is more oriented to the relationship. A man wants physical connection; the woman desires an emotional connection. Sight, smell, and the physical body stimulate a man. Touch, attitudes, actions, words, and the whole person stimulate the woman. The woman needs to be understood, loved, and needed emotionally, along with time to warm up to the sexual act. As Isabel Allende writes in her book, *Of Love and Shadows*: "For women, the best aphrodisiacs are words. The G-spot is in the ears. He who looks for it below there is wasting his time."

The man's sexual response can happen anytime, anywhere. The woman goes through times when she is more interested in sex than others. A man responds sexually by getting excited quickly, while the woman is much slower. She needs warming up, emotional connection, and a feeling of safety. During sex, a man is single-minded, while the woman might be easily distracted by wondering about the children, the doors, the noise outside, or other minor things going on around them.

And when it comes to sexual satisfaction or release, there are differences as well. A man's orgasm is more intense and shorter, while a woman's is longer and comprises more depth. A man generally requires the orgasm for sexual fulfillment while a woman may not need it at all (although I'm sure she'd rather have one than not!).

One of the common issues for men (at least those we've spoken with) is a tendency for sexual selfishness. With that singular focus we mentioned above, there is a natural drive to satisfy his own need without satisfying that of the woman. It's not malicious but again is due to a lack of understanding the woman and miscommunicating each other's needs.

For many couples, talking about sex is not easy, especially if your Friendship is still growing. But by getting vulnerable and a little uncomfortable, the following steps can help you bridge the connection gap in the bedroom. The best sex comes when you communicate about it. If you still feel like you need some help, there are many sex therapists the two of you can see together that can specifically help you overcome many challenges.

Tell the truth.

Tell your partner the truth about how you feel about your sex life together. If you want more frequency, ask for it. If you want more foreplay, make sure you talk about it. The second meaning is to tell the truth about your experience: if you have trouble having an orgasm because you need more foreplay, be honest about that. If you need more kissing before sex, say so. Telling the truth means being honest about what you need sexually and having a discussion with your partner about it.

Ask for what you want.

This could sound like:

- "I wanted to tell you that I would like more foreplay when we are sexual before we have intercourse."

- "I really need more kissing and touching outside the bedroom before we just start touching sexually in the bedroom."

- "I want us to experiment with different positions in bed, rather than the same position we always use."

Really asking for what you want is a huge step toward having a better and more fulfilling sexual relationship. Remember, couples that have great sex do so because they have talked about it. Great sex ends up happening when you ask for what you want because it's a more fulfilling experience.

Let go.

Letting go of inhibitions is a great way to make your sex better. This could mean trying to relax more during intimacy. It could mean letting go of ideas about "the way sex is supposed to look." It could be trying a new kind of foreplay you haven't experimented with or haven't done with your partner in a long time. Letting go could also mean that you experiment with having sex with a different script, such as kissing then intercourse then foreplay. Find out how your mate likes to be touched. Letting your inhibitions with your partner go can be a wonderful way to connect, build intimacy, and strengthen your relationship.

Prioritize your sex life.

Things that have priority in your life get accomplished. If you set a goal to eat better, you are likely to be more aware of your food. If you set a goal to get more sleep, you'll go to bed earlier. If you set a goal to have a better physical relationship, you will invest more time in it. This is exactly what we do in our marriage. When we feel like our sexual intimacy is on a decline, we schedule it. We do sex challenges (like a five-day sex challenge) to get us back on track. We also go to bed at the same time. By going to bed together, you then increase the opportunity for touching, talking, kissing, and sex in the relationship overall.

Remember, creating a life as Lovers is the pinnacle. It can be the most uncomfortable to cultivate, but it's also the most rewarding. Remember to consistently work on and check in with your Partnership and nurture your fondness in Friendship. When there are challenges with being Lovers, maximizing these other elements will make it that much easier for the two of you to get back on track. The solid foundation of your relationship home makes replacing a few shingles after a storm seems like easy work.

SECTION IV:
BECOME A LEGENDARY COUPLE

— 11 —
BECOMING A LEGENDARY COUPLE

"Whether you think you can or you think you can't,
you're right."

—HENRY FORD

So now that we've given you a lot of information in this book, what do you do now? While we've said that this book is the beginning of a journey, we want to be sure that you're left with the tools to go much further than that. Below we will give you a framework from which the two of you can begin working. Not only does it create a roadmap of ideas and questions you can incorporate into your Miracle Morning for Couples routine, but these steps can be used during any intentional date night you might have, or even a purposeful weekend getaway. The two of us still use it as a guide today as we adjust and pivot the vision we've created for our marriage and family.

As you go through it, think about all the Four Legendary Relationship Elements. What would it look and feel like if you were experiencing level 10 in all four areas: a thriving You, successful Partners, committed Friends, and deep, intimate Lovers?

We're cheering you on! You've got this!

Christopher and Kari Lochhead

We sat down and had a very candid and spirited conversation with Christopher and Kari Lochhead about their marriage and relationships in general. Christopher is a best-selling author and host of the *Christopher Lochhead Follow Your Different* podcast and Kari is a successful event planner and real-estate developer and designer.

We wanted to be sure to talk with them about the way that they intentionally designed their legendary relationship and how they consciously *choose* how they show up for each other. We have always admired their relationship. They have a rare connection that is raw, authentic, honest, and extremely playful... and they didn't get there by accident.

[KL]: "Both of us really wanted to be in a great relationship."

They designed it from the very beginning. They talked about the big things—they had the big, important conversations—even before they moved in together. Things like, 'Are we going to have children, where are we going to live, how are we going to handle finances, and what are our core values?'

[KL]: "You have to get the big stuff right first. This is my lifestyle. 'Do you want to live this way? Great, because I want to live this way.' Things don't happen naturally. Things happen because you want them to happen. If I don't like his way of life or his way of thinking, then we're doomed."

The two of them are incredibly direct about how they intentionally design their relationship.

Because they had the important conversations about the big things, it allowed them to be in alignment with each other from the beginning. When that stage is set, the small things (that might bother them) mattered so much less. In fact, they told us that the small things really don't matter at all. They made an intentional choice to avoid the nitpicking that can happen in relationships altogether.

[CL]: "You have to *know* who you are married to, whether it's about the big stuff or even the small stuff."

[KL]: "I don't care that Christopher doesn't rinse out the sink after brushing his teeth."

[CL]: "Wait, this is the first time I've ever heard about this."

[KL]: "We don't fight about that because it doesn't actually matter. I don't care that he doesn't put the cap on the toothpaste. I don't care if he puts the toilet paper on the wrong way. This is the majority of what people fight about. Who cares? Who cares about that stuff? What becomes the problem is the bad feelings from the ongoing report card. Who wants that?"

And that's the end of it. But if things do get tough - when the challenges present themselves- Christopher and Kari have a beautiful way of navigating it.

When they start to get heated, maybe even angry, they say, "*That's Not Us!*" It's their safe word, their mantra, for ending the battle before it even gets started. But they don't simply ignore it. They wait until the emotion has passed so they can have a constructive talk about it.

[CL]: "If it's a big thing, we wait until later and talk about it… if it's a small thing, then who cares?"

Another big part of their marriage design is the way they show up for each other… how they support and encourage each other. What other couples might see as a compromise, the two of them see as a way to show that encouragement… to support what lights the other up or makes them happy.

[CL]: "My job is to empower Kari's awesomeness, her genius, and to support it. It's the greatest feeling to me to see her on fire."

[KL]: "And I also *know* what he looks like to be on fire. I know what he gets excited about when he is at his personal best, and I make sure to help him reach that point."

These things help them show each other that they have the other's back… that they're on the same team. They highlight how important this is, that the other knows it. And this support continues even when they might be apart.

[CL]: "I've learned something from Kari's father that is always in my frontal lobe. I watch her dad with her mom, and Phil is *always* on Jean's side. Always. It doesn't matter what it is. Even if they don't agree. Even if she is at odds with another person. Phil's on Jean's side. Period. And you can't say anything bad about her in front of Phil. And so, I'm always on Kari's side. Always."

There's no talking behind the other's back.

[KL]: "The things I talk about Christopher to my girlfriends about, he already knows. We've already talked about it. I mean, I might joke to them about how loud he is. He knows that!"

[CL]: "Bix Bickson says it very powerfully. He says, 'The real definition of love is when you are loved for exactly who you *are* and exactly for who you *are not.*'"

This line goes a long way regarding who Christopher and Kari have decided who they want to be in their marriage.

[KL]: "Let's just love each other through it. I love him that he makes a huge mess across the entire counter just to make one piece of toast. I actually love him for that. And if I just *choose* that to be true... how I react is a choice. How I love him is a choice. Always. And when I choose to love him for that, then how can we ever fight about it?"

[CL]: "And you know... now that I know about the sink thing, I'll choose to get better about that, too."

STEP 1: VISION

"The only thing worse than being blind
is having sight but no vision."

—HELEN KELLER, American author, political activist,
and lecturer

Legendary couples know where they are going, and they know what they are working toward.

You don't get in the car without a destination, or you will end up somewhere you don't want to be: in the wrong location. That's exactly what happens when you don't know where you are going with your relationship. We are not going to let that happen this time! We are taking control of our destination. We are going to clearly see the direction we are heading.

Begin by individually thinking about what "legendary" means to you in all four of your Relationship Elements: You, Partners, Friends, Lovers. Go through each of them and ask yourself the following questions:

1. When has this element been at its best?

2. When have you been most proud of your accomplishments together?

3. What are the actions and habits you contributed during those times?

4. How do you show up when you are at your best?

5. Describe what this element would look like in your relationship if it were a level 10?

6. What would your relationship look and feel like in one year if it were legendary?

Your answers can be as deep or as simple as you want when you start.

Once you have spent some time investigating your personal vision for the elements, discuss it as a couple to begin to put your shared vision together.

Your answers will leave clues about what works naturally for you and what doesn't. You will see similarities in stories and desires. You will see the differences. All of this is okay.

Work back and forth, and begin to create a vision that feels right to both of you. Some things will come easy; there will be obvious things that you agree on and important aspects that you both want to bring back into the relationship. And there may be things that you don't agree on or are unsure about. It is important for you to both remember that you are in this relationship together. If one or both of you are in this relationship for only you, your Partnership won't form properly. When you are both in it for the health of your relationship, you ultimately get what you both want: two happy people, thriving and in love. It is not necessary to iron out every detail on your first discussion. Know that this part of the process is ever evolving. As you grow individually and as a couple, your vision will progress. Revisit this step as often as you can, whether it's once a year, twice a year, quarterly, or monthly. Reviewing it is just as important as creating it.

STEP 2: GOALS

"I have found, over and over, that a person of average intelligence with clear goals will run circles around a genius who is not sure what he or she really wants."

—BRIAN TRACY, motivational public speaker
and self-development author

Now that you have a vision that you have created together, decide on the most important things to tackle first. Remember the Relationship Elements pyramid and start with the foundation of the You Element and the Partners Element if there are things that need work in these areas. We want a solid foundation for a lifelong legendary relationship. So, start at the foundation and work your way up. Select 1 to 3 goals to work on at a time. What would make the most impact? Start there and write them down.

STEP 3: PLAN

"A goal without a plan is just a wish."

—ANTOINE DE SAINT-EXUP*É*RY

We cannot stress enough (again) that a plan is vitally important in your intimate relationship. Without a plan, we get stuck in the Partnership Loop of resentment, power struggles, and disconnection.

Plans are critical. They are the roadmap that tells you how to get to your destination. They give you the steps and habits that you need to make your vision a reality. They also help you take the right actions in the right order and help ensure that you don't miss critical steps. As for how to plot your plan, you can use any effective planning system. If you have one that works for you, use that! Just get started by reverse engineering your vision and getting clear on the actions, habits, tools, and resources you need to get there. Here are basic steps to create a plan:

1. Brainstorm—Grab a clean sheet of paper and write down all of the things you can think of that will make your goal a reality. What are the actions, habits, resources, people, and tools that would or could help you get there? Write them down.

2. Organize your brainstorm list into the following four categories:

   a. Action Steps

   b. Habits

   c. People

   d. Tools/Resources

3. Prioritize—What is the first action you can take to move this forward? What comes next? Create a step-by-step list of what to do.

Remember the power in making your initial habits for the plan "stupid small" at first. This makes them more achievable, sets the habits in motion, creates a compound effect, and guides and leads you to bigger dreams and goals in the future.

STEP 4: CREATE SPACE

"What distracts us will begin to define us. We don't need to swing at every pitch."

—BOB GOFF, diplomat and author

"If I had a dollar for every time I got distracted, I wish I had a puppy."

—UNKNOWN

We live in the most distracted era of all time, and our happiness (or lack thereof) reflects that fact, unfortunately. Bringing awareness to the things that derail us is a seemingly simple step that will yield a lot of opportunities. There are things like receiving consistent phone notifications, simply grabbing our phone whenever there is a pause in life and saying yes to something when you don't actually have the time.

Following are multiple areas in which we can find ourselves distracted.

Electronics

The overuse of electronics is one of the most common causes of relationship dissatisfaction and partner complaint. It is no wonder people feel "out of balance;" our devices are affecting every area of our lives because they are portable enough to go everywhere we go and are designed to keep our attention. Sadly, if most people tracked the amount of time our electronics received our undivided attention instead of our partner, we would be mortified (but probably not surprised). We struggled with this in the beginning, so we downloaded apps that tracked how much time we were spending on social media and other distractions. It also told us how often we picked up our phones throughout the day. On the first day, Brandy picked up her phone 167 times. Consider what would happen to our relationship if she grabbed Lance's hand 167 times per day instead! She also had the Instagram app running for over an hour and a half. Let's look at how much time that could be:

1.5 hours/day x 365 days/year x 25 years = 13,687.5 hours

They say it takes 10,000 hours to master something. Scrolling Instagram isn't mastering anything, and it definitely isn't mastering the most important relationship sitting right in front of her.

Darren Hardy, in his book *The Compound Effect*, said, "What stands between you and your goal is your behavior. Do you need to stop doing anything, so the Compound Effect isn't taking you into a downward spiral? Similarly, what do you need to start doing to change your trajectory so that it's headed in the most beneficial direction? In other words, what habits and behaviors do you need to subtract from and add to your life? Your life comes down to this formula:

YOU → CHOICE (decision) + BEHAVIOR (action) + HABIT + COMPOUNDED (repeated action x time) = GOALS

"That's why it's imperative to figure out which behaviors are blocking the path that leads to your goal, and which behaviors help you accomplish your goal."

We can choose to compound our distractions and go further down a path of unhappiness, or we can choose to compound the actions to get us to where we want to be.

Systems

Just as we discussed in the YOU section, another way to create space is to create systems for things you do together. Notice patterns and things you repeatedly do in your life, such as ongoing requirements and activities for the kids, regular grocery items, and everyday chores. How can you create systems that make these things efficient? What time of day will you do them? How much time will you devote to getting them done? Create your system or checklists and keep them consistent.

Leverage

If you live a busy life, you may need to bring in some help, even if it is temporary. This will take some financial investment, but think of what your time is worth in terms of keeping your marriage intact. Can you delegate house cleaning to a third party so that you can do more relationship-boosting activities? The reason why the virtual assistant business is thriving is that savvy people are thinking about leverage. They want the time back to do the things that bring them joy or make them money. This is important to consider in a time of transition. When you are just getting started with adding in more time for your relationship, and you haven't hit your stride, consider buying some time, literally. If you're still not convinced, think of it this way: by allowing someone to help you, you are helping to feed another family.

STEP 5: COMMIT

"Discipline is the bridge between goals and accomplishment."

—JIM ROHN

The more disciplined you get about the things that improve your life, the easier it all becomes. Life will begin to click and work; it will become legendary. Once you have identified the actions that take you away from your goals and those that bring you closer, it is time to go all in. For this section, we are going to bring in one of our favorite minds, Brian Johnson from Optimize.me.

Brian Johnson says in one of his +1 videos, "Making a 100% commitment is surprisingly way easier than a 90% commitment or even a 99.9% commitment. There is something about going all in 100% on a commitment that saves a ton of energy and makes it way more likely to stick. The fact is when we have anything less than a total 100% commitment, we've made room for that little whiny voice to come in and start negotiating with us right when we can least afford it and when we most need to ignore it."

We couldn't agree more! We not only sacrifice time and momentum when we take our eye off the prize, but we also fall behind and are forced to jump back into the race. It will happen, and we will talk about how to prepare for it later, but this is not the goal. Our mission is to create a legendary relationship, so we are committing to making it happen.

Brian also talks about Barry Michels' and Phil Stutz's excellent book, *Coming Alive*, which talks about the two parts inside all of us: the Dreamer and the Doer.

Brian teaches, "Self-restraint is what creates true confidence, for a couple of reasons. First, if you don't have self-restraint and you allow yourself to get carried away by every impulse you have, you never know when your life is going to go off the rails. And second, if you don't have the self-mastery to do what you say is important, you never know if you will actually follow through on the big dreams you have. That's where the Dreamer and Doer come in. Your Dreamer is the version of you that can see your infinite potential; it knows you can do so much more than you are currently doing. Your Doer is the part of you that actually does the things that are best for you. Your Dreamer needs to be able to trust your Doer. Your Dreamer needs to know that when you say something is important, your Doer will rock it. If you don't have that confidence in your Doer, you won't have the confidence it takes to rock it."

He then reminds us that the Latin root for the word *confidence* literally means *intense trust*. In this case, we are talking about the trust between your Dreamer and Doer. Thank you, Brian!

STEP 6: TAKE ACTION

"The key is to start NOW. Every great act, every fantastic adventure, starts with small steps. The first step always looks harder than it actually is."

—DARREN HARDY, American author, keynote speaker, advisor, and former publisher

Grant Cardone says in his book, *The 10x Rule*, "Exactly how much action is necessary to create success?" Not surprisingly, everyone is looking for the secret shortcut, and equally unsurprising is the following fact: there are no shortcuts. The more action you take, the better your chances are of getting a break. Disciplined, consistent, and persistent actions are more of a determining factor in the creation of success than any other combination of things. Understanding how to calculate the necessary steps and then take the right amount of action is more important than your concept, idea, invention, or plan. Most people fail only because they are operating at the wrong degree of action. To simplify action, we are going to break down your choices into four simple categories, or degrees, of action. Your four choices are:

1. Do nothing.

2. Retreat.

3. Take normal levels of action.

4. Take massive action.

Most people live in the first three degrees of action: they either do nothing, retreat, or take normal levels of action. Those who achieve their desires are the ones taking huge leaps of massive action.

Kind of sounds a bit like "suck" (do nothing/retreat), "don't suck" (take normal action), or "legendary" (take massive action), right?

We are not looking for normal levels of success! We are not looking for "don't suck" levels of success. We want legendary success! This is only possible if we do the work.

In *The Compound Effect*, Darren Hardy said, "The same thing happens when a rocket ship launches. The space shuttle uses more fuel during the first few minutes of its flight than it does the rest of the entire trip. Why? Because it has to break free from the pull of gravity. Once it does, it can glide in orbit. The hard part? Getting off the ground. Your old ways and your old conditioning are just like the inertia of the merry-go-round or the pull of gravity. Everything just wants to stay at rest. You'll need a lot of energy to break your inertia and get your new enterprise under way. But once you get momentum, you will be hard to stop—virtually unbeatable—even though you're now putting out considerably less effort while receiving greater results."

It's also like going to the gym or beginning a workout; just getting started is the hardest part! Once you're in it, you enjoy it, especially when you're done and feeling great. Have you ever said after a workout, "Boy, I wish I hadn't done that!"? Us neither.

Your T.E.A.M. time could be viewed the same. It's not easy to get started, but if it helps, think about the fact that you have a built-in accountability partner with your mate. The two of you can encourage and inspire each other to take massive action on yourselves and your relationship.

In no time, you will gain momentum, feel victorious, and then be motivated to add more commitments and habits that will move your relationship forward like never before.

STEP 7: CHECK IN

"People who use time wisely spend it on activities that advance their overall purpose in life."

— JOHN C. MAXWELL,

No one has time to do the wrong thing for too long. Effective checking in will propel your success. If you are not checking in, you can expect your success to suffer. It is the step that allows you to stop and say, "Hey this is working; let's continue or do more of it," or, "This isn't working; let's stop and try something new." We think it is so important that checking in become part of your morning together in T.E.A.M.

When checking in, talk about what is working and what isn't working. Make adjustments along the way. As with any other type of plan, it's perfectly normal to remove something that just isn't serving your relationship. But again, the key to this is talking about it ... a.k.a. *checking in!*

A simple way to do this at any time is to share where you are on a scale of 1-10 in any element or with any action you are taking. You might ask your partner, "From 1-10, how are you feeling about our Friendship?" Or, "On a scale of 1-10 how am I doing on actively listening to you this week?"

Be sure to also schedule your weekly check-ins. These don't always have to be during date night but having agreed-upon moments to check in gets both of you ready and in the frame of mind to share and discuss. After the kids go to bed or even during your morning coffee are great times to get out the commitments section and share.

Use your meeting time during T.E.A.M. for this. Often during our weekly check-in, we create a list of discussion topics, then use our meeting time to tackle them each day, one by one. We're never short on things on which to check in.

STEP 8: RESET

"Failing to Plan is Planning to fail."

—ALAN LAKEIN, author

You must be ready for things to get off track and someone to mess up. We are human and live very complicated lives. The longer you sit in anger, frustration, or overwhelm, the harder it is to get back on track. One of the beautiful things about having a vision and a plan in place is the ability to grab it, see how much progress you've made, check in with each other, and reset! Start again. Get back to it. Plan for a reset!

The key to a proper reset, especially before you do it, is to have grace. Things happen. You can get sick, maybe you're moving homes, whatever it may be –life happens! Big events create big priorities and big changes. Recognize this, and have grace. In fact, the writing of this book you're reading took place (mostly) in the wee hours of the morning, and many times it cut into our own S.A.V.E.R.S. and T.E.A.M. time. But we know it's for a season. We have grace, and we know we'll be back to it regularly soon.

CELEBRATE

"The more you praise and celebrate your life, the more there is to celebrate."

—OPRAH WINFREY, American media executive, actress, talk show host, television producer, and philanthropist

You must celebrate along the way!

Why? Because any accomplishment, no matter how small, activates the reward circuitry of our brains. When this pathway is opened, some key chemicals are released that give us a feeling of achievement and pride.

In particular, a neurotransmitter called dopamine is released, which energizes us and gives us a feel-good aura. This chemical enables us not only to get that sweet feeling of reward but also to take action to move toward what triggered its release in the first place.

Darren Hardy says, "All work and no play is a recipe for backsliding."

Working on yourself and your relationship is a wonderful thing and should be celebrated as such.

No matter how little the victory or event, they're all worth taking time to reflect on the moment. When you follow through on commitments, have an amazing talk, or resurrect some lost intimacy … celebrate! High five, go on a date, laugh together, or spend some time together as a family. Celebrate it all; you are creating a deep and lasting connection together as a couple!

THE BEST IS YET TO COME!

Hal and Ursula Elrod

Creating a legendary relationship is a cornerstone of this book. What that looks like to each person can be different. We must define it for ourselves. And so, we were lucky enough to sit down and talk with Hal and Ursula about the definition of 'legendary' and what that means to each of *them* for their marriage.

[UE]: "For me, a legendary relationship is two people who have chosen to create a family of their own, where divorce is not an option. You show up for each other, always, and you show your children what a healthy relationship looks like. When we kiss in the kitchen, and the kids say 'eww,' I tell them that they should actually be scared of a day that doesn't happen. Legendary is having a relationship that other people look at and say, 'I would like something like that, too.' It's not by any means perfect. There is no perfect relationship. Hal can attest to that. We have dealt with our fair share or stress and struggles that challenged the strength of our relationship. From losing a house, having to move in with Hal's dad, w/our newborn, because we couldn't even get approved to rent something, leaving our family behind and moving to a completely new state, and Hal being diagnosed with cancer. All of this craziness. It's never perfect.

So, I think for me the biggest thing is that, if there's a real problem in the relationship, but you're just tired and you don't want to struggle or put in extraordinary effort into making it good again... that's not enough of a reason to leave. I'm sorry, the beautiful things come out of that struggle. Nothing worth having was ever gained easily. The caterpillar has to struggle out of the cocoon to become a butterfly. Life and marriage are a struggle, too. No one is without struggle in this life, but that is where growth and magic happen, getting through the hard things. For us, divorce is not a word that will ever enter any type of argument between us. We just don't bring that up. That's not fair, it's a low blow in my opinion. Now, I can be mean for sure.... but that is one big rule we have. We made a deal, when we fight, we fight fair.

It's going to be messy and it's going to be ugly. But it's also going to be fun and it's going to be an adventure. Marriage is such an amazing journey in life, one of the best I've ever been on, and there's still a lot of this adventure left ahead of us. If do you feel stuck, if it starts to feel old, if it begins to feel like the grass is greener on the other side, rather than 'selling the house to get a new yard', start putting effort into your yard. It can get beautiful and green again, it just takes hard work sometimes.

[HE]: "I feel like a legendary relationship is two people that are coming from a place of unconditional love and really supporting each other in being the best version of ourselves. I read a book when in my early to mid-20's called *The Mastery of Love* by Don Miguel Ruiz, who also wrote *The Four Agreements*. He speaks to that. He says love is wanting for another person what they want for themselves. Most of us are very selfish in relationships. 'I want you to do this, I want you to be this way, I want your time, you need to spend more time with me, and you need to do it right.' I want a relationship where we're loving each other and supporting what the other wants. We help each other to achieve that experience, goal, or desire and support them in becoming their highest best self.

What's cool is when Ursula and I were first dating, she was at my house, and of all the books on the shelf (you know there were hundreds of books) she picks that book up. She says, 'what's this book all about'. I reply, 'That's the book that defines love in the way that I would define it. Whatever woman I eventually marry has to have read that book and be in agreement with it. Because that's going to be a foundational part of our relationship'. And she says, "Can I borrow it?' That was a great sign for our relationship.

So, deciding that you're going to show up in your relationship to serve the other person selflessly. That's what a legendary relationship is to me."

— 12 —
THE MIRACLE MORNING 30-DAY LIFE TRANSFORMATION CHALLENGE

"An extraordinary life is all about daily, continuous improvements in the areas that matter most."

—ROBIN SHARMA, Canadian writer

Let's play devil's advocate for a moment. Can The Miracle Morning really transform any area of your life, or relationship, in just 30 days? Can anything really make *that* significant of an impact, that quickly? Well, remember that it has already brought change for thousands of others, and if it works for them, it can and absolutely will work for you.

Incorporating or changing any habit requires an acclimation period, so don't expect this to be effortless from day one. However, by making a commitment to yourself to stick with this challenge, beginning each day with a Miracle Morning and leveraging the S.A.V.E.R.S. will quickly become the foundational habit that makes all others possible. Remember: *win the morning, and you set yourself up to win the day.*

The seemingly unbearable first few days of changing a habit are only temporary. While there's a lot of debate about how long it takes to implement a new habit, there is a powerful 3-phase strategy that has proven successful for the hundreds of thousands of individuals who have learned how to conquer the snooze button and who now wake up every day for their Miracle Morning.

From Unbearable to Unstoppable:

The 3-Phase Strategy to Implement Any Habit in 30 Days

As you take The Miracle Morning 30-Day Life Transformation Challenge, we'll share with you arguably the simplest and most effective strategy for implementing and sustaining any new habit, in just 30 days. This will give you the mindset and approach to build your new routine.

Phase One: Unbearable (Days 1–10)

Phase One is when any new activity requires the most amount of conscious effort, and getting up early is no different. You're fighting existing habits, the very habits that have been entrenched in *who you are* for years.

In this phase, it's mind over matter—and if you don't mind, it'll definitely matter! The habit of hitting the snooze button and not making the most of your day are the same habits that hold you back from becoming the superstar partner you have always known you can be. So, dig in and hold strong.

In Phase One, while you battle existing patterns and limiting beliefs, you'll find out what you're made of and what you're capable of. You need to keep pushing, stay committed to your vision, and hang in there. Trust us when we say you can do this!

We know it can be daunting on day five to realize you still have twenty-five days to go before your transformation is complete and you've become a bona fide morning person. Keep in mind that on day five, you're more than halfway through the first phase and well on your way. Remember: your initial feelings are not going to last forever. In fact, you owe it to yourself to persevere because, in no time at all, you'll be getting the exact results you want as you become the person you've always wanted to be!

Phase Two: Uncomfortable (Days 11–20)

In Phase Two, your body and mind begin to acclimate to waking up earlier. You'll notice that getting up starts to feel a tiny bit easier, but it's not yet a habit—it's not quite who you are and likely won't feel natural yet.

The biggest temptation at this level is to reward yourself by taking a break, especially on the weekends. A question posted quite often in The Miracle Morning Community is, "How many days a week do you get up early for your Miracle Morning?" Our answer—and the one that's most common from longtime Miracle Morning practitioners—is *every single day*.

Once you've made it through Phase One, you're past the hardest period. Keep going! Why on earth would you want to go through that first phase again by taking one or two days off? Trust us, you wouldn't, so don't!

Phase Three: Unstoppable (Days 21–30)

Early rising is now not only a habit, but it has also literally become part of *who you are*, part of your identity. Your body and mind will have become accustomed to your new way of being. These next ten days are important for cementing the habit in yourself and your life.

As you engage in The Miracle Morning practice, you will also develop an appreciation for the three distinct phases of habit change. A side benefit is that you will realize you can identify, develop, and adopt any habit that serves you—including the habits of exceptional *relationships* that we have included in this book.

Now that you've learned the simplest and most effective strategy for successfully implementing and sustaining any new habit in 30 days, you know the mindset and approach that you need to complete The Miracle Morning 30-Day Transformation Challenge. All that's required is for you to commit to get started and then follow through.

Consider the Rewards

When you commit to The Miracle Morning 30-Day Transformation Challenge, you will be building a foundation for success in every area of your life, for the rest of your life. By waking up each morning and practicing your Miracle Morning, you will begin each day with extraordinary levels of **discipline** (the crucial ability to get yourself to follow through with your commitments), **clarity** (the power you'll generate from focusing on what's most important), and **personal development** (perhaps the single most significant determining factor in your success). Thus, in the next thirty days, you'll find yourself quickly *becoming the person* you need to be to create the extraordinary levels of personal, professional, and financial success you truly desire.

You'll also be transforming The Miracle Morning from a concept that you may be excited (and possibly a little nervous) to "try" into a lifelong habit, one that will continue to develop you into the person you need to be to create the life you've always wanted. You'll begin to fulfill your potential and see results in your life far beyond what you've ever experienced before.

In addition to developing successful habits, you'll also be developing the **mindset** you need to improve your life—both internally and externally. By practicing the Life S.A.V.E.R.S. each day, you'll be experiencing the physical, intellectual, emotional, and spiritual benefits of *Silence, Affirmations, Visualization, Exercise, Reading,* and *Scribing*. You'll immediately feel less stressed, more centered, more focused, happier and more excited about your life. You'll be generating more energy, clarity, and motivation to move toward your highest goals and dreams (especially those you've been putting off for far too long).

Remember, your life situation will improve after—but only *after*—you develop yourself into the person you need to be to improve it. That's exactly what these next thirty days of your life can be—a new beginning, and a new you.

You Can Do This!

If you're feeling nervous, hesitant, or concerned about whether or not you will be able to follow through with this for thirty days, relax—it's completely normal to feel that way. This is especially true if waking up in the morning is something you've found challenging in the past. It's not only expected that you would be a bit hesitant or nervous, but it's actually a very good sign! It's a sign that you're *ready* to commit. Otherwise you wouldn't be nervous.

Here's how to get started.

Step 1: Get The Miracle Morning 30-Day Transformation Challenge Fast Start Kit.

Visit www.TMMBook.com to download your free Miracle Morning 30-Day Life Transformation Challenge Fast Start Kit—complete with exercises, affirmations, daily checklists, tracking sheets, and everything else you need to make starting and completing The Miracle Morning 30-Day Life Transformation Challenge as easy as possible. Please take a minute to do this now.

Step 2: Plan Your First Miracle Morning for Tomorrow.

If you haven't already, commit to (and schedule) your first Miracle Morning as soon as possible—ideally *tomorrow*. Yes, actually write it into your schedule and decide where it will take place. Remember, it's recommended that you leave your bedroom and remove yourself from the temptations of your bed altogether. Our Miracle Morning takes place every day on our living room couch while everyone else in our house is still sound asleep. We've heard from people who do their Miracle Morning sitting outside in nature, such as on their porch or deck, or at a nearby park. Do yours where you feel most comfortable, but also where you won't be interrupted.

Step 3: Read Page One of the Fast Start Kit and Do the Exercises.

Read the introduction in your Miracle Morning 30-Day Life Transformation Challenge Fast Start Kit, and then please follow the instructions and complete the exercises. Like anything in life that's worthwhile, successfully completing The Miracle Morning 30-Day Life Transformation Challenge requires a bit of preparation. It's important that you do the initial exercises in your Fast Start Kit (which shouldn't take you more than an hour) and keep in mind that your

Miracle Morning will always start with the *preparation* you do the day or night before to get yourself ready mentally, emotionally, and logistically for your Miracle Morning. This preparation includes following the steps in the Five-Step Snooze-Proof Wake-Up Strategy covered in chapter two.

Step 3.1: Get an Accountability Partner (Recommended).

The overwhelming evidence for the correlation between success and accountability is undeniable. While most people resist being held accountable, it is hugely beneficial to have someone who will hold us to higher standards than we'll hold ourselves to. All of us can benefit from the support of an accountability partner, so it's highly recommended—but definitely not required—that you reach out to someone in your circle of influence (family, friend, colleague, significant other, etc.) and invite them to join you in The Miracle Morning 30-Day Life Transformation Challenge.

Not only does having someone to hold us accountable increase the odds that we will follow through, but joining forces with someone else is simply more fun! Consider that when you're excited about something and committed to doing it on your own, there is a certain level of power in that excitement and in your individual commitment. However, when you have someone else in your life—a friend, family member, or co-worker—who's as excited about and committed to it as you are, it's much more powerful.

Call, text, or email one or more people today, and invite them to join you for The Miracle Morning 30-Day Life Transformation Challenge. The quickest way to get them up to speed is to send them the link to www.MiracleMorning.com so they can get free and immediate access to The Miracle Morning Fast Start Kit, including:

➡ **The FREE Miracle Morning video training**

➡ **The FREE Miracle Morning audio training**

➡ **Two FREE chapters of *The Miracle Morning* book**

It will cost them nothing, and you'll be teaming up with someone who is also committed to taking their life to the next level so the two of you can support and encourage one another, while also holding each other accountable.

IMPORTANT: Don't wait until you have an accountability partner on board to do your first Miracle Morning and start the 30-Day Life Transformation Challenge. Whether or not you've found someone to embark on the journey with you, I still recommend scheduling and doing your first Miracle Morning tomorrow—no matter what. Don't wait. You'll be even more capable of inspiring someone else to do The Miracle Morning with you if you've already experienced a few days of it. Get started. Then, as soon as you can, invite a friend, family member, or co-worker to visit www.MiracleMorning.com to get their free Miracle Morning Fast Start Kit.

In less than an hour, they'll be fully capable of being your Miracle Morning accountability partner—not to mention probably a little inspired.

Are You Ready To Take *Your* Life To the Next Level?

What is the next level in your personal or professional life? Which areas need to be transformed for you to reach that level? Give yourself the gift of investing just thirty days to make significant improvements in your life, one day at a time. No matter what your past has been, you *can* change your future by changing the present.

— CONCLUSION —

Let Today Be the Day You Give Up Who You've Been for Who You Can Become

"Every day, think as you wake up, 'Today I am fortunate to have woken up, I am alive, I have a precious human life, I am not going to waste it. I am going to use all my energies to develop myself, to expand my heart out to others. I am going to benefit others as much as I can."

—DALAI LAMA, Buddhist monk

"Things do not change. We change."

—HENRY DAVID THOREAU, American essayist,
poet, philosopher,

Where you are is a result of who you *were*, but where you go from here depends entirely on who you choose to be, from this moment forward.

Now is your time. Decide that today is the most important day of your life because it is who you are becoming now—based on the choices that you make and the actions that you take—which will determine who and where you are going to be for the rest of your life. Don't put off creating and experiencing the life—full of happiness, health, wealth, success, and love—that you truly want and deserve.

As one of my mentors, Kevin Bracy always urged: "Don't wait to be great." If you want your life to improve, you have to improve yourself first. You can start by downloading The Miracle Morning 30-Day Life Transformation Fast-Start Kit at www.TMMBook.com. Then, with or without an accountability partner, commit to completing your 30-day challenge so that you will immediately begin accessing more of your potential than you ever have before. Imagine … just one month from now, you will be well on your way to transforming every area of your life.

Let's Keep Helping Others

May I ask you a quick favor?

If this book has added value to your life, if you feel like you're better off after reading it, and you see that The Miracle Morning can be a new beginning for you to take any—or every—area of your life to the next level, I'm hoping you'll do something for someone you care about.

That simple action is to give this book to them. Let them borrow your copy. Ask them to read it so they have the opportunity to transform their life for the better. Or, if you're not willing to give up your copy quite yet because you're planning on going back and re-reading it, maybe get them their own copy, it could be for no special occasion at all, other than to say, "Hey, I love and appreciate you, and I want to help you live your best life. Read this."

If you believe, as I do, that being a great friend (or family member) is about helping your friends and loved ones to become the best versions of themselves, I encourage you to share this book with them.

Together, we are truly elevating the consciousness of humanity, one morning at a time.

Thank you so much.

A SPECIAL INVITATION FROM HAL

Readers and practitioners of *The Miracle Morning* have co-created an extraordinary community consisting of over 180,000+ like-minded individuals from around the world who wake up each day *with purpose* and dedicate time to fulfilling the unlimited potential that is within all of us, while helping others to do the same.

As the author of *The Miracle Morning*, I felt that I had a responsibility to create an online community where readers could come together to connect, get encouragement, share best practices, support one another, discuss the book, post videos, find accountability partners, and even swap smoothie recipes and exercise routines.

However, I honestly had no idea that The Miracle Morning Community would become one of the most positive, engaged, and supportive online communities in the world, but it has. I'm constantly astounded by the caliber and the character of our members, which presently includes people from over 70 countries and is growing daily.

To join the Miracle Morning Community, just go to **MyTM-MCommunity.com** and request to join The Miracle Morning Community on Facebook. You'll immediately be able to connect with 180,000+ people who are already practicing TMM. While you'll find many who are just beginning their Miracle Morning journey, you'll find even more who have been at it for years and who will happily share advice, support, and guidance to accelerate your success.

I moderate the Community and check in regularly, so I look forward to seeing you there! If you'd like to connect with me personally on social media, just follow **@HalElrod** on Twitter and **Facebook. com/YoPalHal** on Facebook®. Let's connect soon!

BONUS CHAPTER
The Miracle Equation
by Hal Elrod

"There are only two ways to live your life.
One is as though nothing is a miracle.
The other is as though everything is a miracle."

—ALBERT EINSTEIN, German-born theoretical physicist

You understand now that you *can* wake up early, maintain extraordinary levels of energy, direct your focus, and master the not-so-obvious You and Together skills from Lance and Brandy. If you also apply what follows to every aspect of your life, you're going to go much further; you're going to make your life truly exceptional.

To make this leap, there is one more helpful tool for you to add to your toolbox, and it's called The Miracle Equation.

The Miracle Equation is the underlying strategy that I used to realize my full potential as a salesperson, as well as a friend, spouse, and parent. And it has to do with how you handle your goals. One of my mentors, Dan Casetta, taught me: "The purpose of a goal isn't to hit the goal. The real purpose is to develop yourself into the type of person who can achieve your goals, regardless of whether you hit that particular one or not. It is who you become by giving it everything you have until the last moment—regardless of your results—that matters most."

When you make the decision to stick with a seemingly unachievable goal, even though the possibility of failure is high, you will become especially focused, faithful, and intentional. When your objective is truly ambitious, it will require you to find out what you are really made of!

Two Decisions

As with any great challenge, you need to make decisions related to achieving the goal. You can set a deadline and then create your own agenda by asking yourself, "If I were to achieve my goal on the deadline, what decisions would I have to make and commit to in advance?"

And you'll find that whatever the goal, the two decisions that would make the biggest impact are *always the same*. They form the basis for The Miracle Equation.

The First Decision: Unwavering Faith

There was a time in my life when I tried to achieve an impossible sales goal. I'll use that as an example to show you what I mean. Though this comes from my sales experience, I'll show you how it applies within the context of your relationship (or any context, really). It was a stressful time, and I was already facing fear and self-doubt, but my thought process about the goal forced me to an important realization: to achieve the seemingly impossible, I would have to maintain unwavering faith every day, *regardless of my results.*

I knew that there would be moments when I would doubt myself and times when I would be so far off track that the goal would no longer seem achievable. But it would be those moments when I would have to override self-doubt with unshakeable faith.

To keep that level of faith in those challenging moments, I repeated what I call my Miracle Mantra:

I will _____ *(reach my goal), no matter what. There is no other option.*

Understand that maintaining unwavering faith isn't *normal.* It's not what most people do. When it doesn't look like the desired result is likely, average performers give up the faith that it's possible. When the game is on the line, a team is down on the scorecards, and there are only seconds left, it is only the top performers—the Michael Jordans of the world—who, without hesitation, tell their team, "Give me the ball."

The rest of the team breathes a sigh of relief because of their fear of missing the game-winning shot, while Michael Jordan made a decision at some point in his life that he would maintain unwavering faith, even though he might miss. (And although Michael Jordan missed twenty-six game-winning shots in his career, his faith that he would make every single one never wavered.)

That's the first decision that very successful people make, and it's yours for the making, too.

When you're working toward a goal, and you're not on track, what is the first thing that goes out the window? *The faith that the outcome you want is possible.* Your self-talk turns negative: *I'm not on track. It doesn't look like I'm going to reach my goal.* And with each passing moment, your faith decreases.

You don't have to settle for that. You have the ability and the choice to maintain that same unwavering faith, no matter what, and regardless of the results. This is key in relationships because results involving other people are often out of your direct control. You may doubt yourself or have a bad day with your partner. In the darkest moments, you wonder if everything will turn out okay. But you must find—over and over again—your faith that all things are possible and hold it throughout your journey, whether it is a five-day sex challenge or a thirty-year marriage goal.

It's very important that you see your role as a spouse as directly related to other high-achieving professions because the parallels are unmistakable. If you don't take time to see the parallels here, you may find that you focus on the failures of your relationship instead of the successes. And if you focus on the failures, your partner likely will too, and that's not what you want. So, stay with me.

Elite athletes maintain unwavering faith that they can make every shot they take. That faith—and the faith you need to develop—isn't based on probability. It comes from a whole different place. Most salespeople operate based on what is known as the *law of averages.* But what we're talking about here is the *law of miracles.* When you miss shot after shot, you must tell yourself what Michael Jordan tells himself: *I've missed three, but I want the ball next, and I'm going to make that next shot.*

And if you miss that one, *your faith doesn't waiver.* You repeat the Miracle Mantra to yourself:

I will _____ (reach my goal), no matter what. There is no other option.

Then, you simply uphold your integrity and do what it is that you say you are going to do.

An elite athlete may be having the worst game ever, where it seems like in the first three-quarters of the game, they can't make a shot to save their life. Yet in the fourth quarter, right when the team needs them, they start making those shots. They always want the ball; they always have belief and faith in themselves. In the fourth quarter, they score three times as many shots as they made in the first three-quarters of the game.

Why? They have conditioned themselves to have unwavering faith in their talents, skills, and abilities, regardless of what it says on the scoreboard or their stats sheet.

And ...

They combine their unwavering faith with part two of The Miracle Equation: extraordinary effort.

The Second Decision: Extraordinary Effort

When you allow your faith to go out the window, effort almost always follows right behind it. *After all,* you tell yourself, *what's the point in even trying to achieve my goal if it's not possible?* Suddenly, you find yourself wondering how you're ever going to feel comfortable touching or flirting with your spouse again, let alone reach the big goal you've been working toward.

I've been there many times, feeling deflated and thinking, *What's the point of even trying?* And you might easily think, *There's no way I can make it. My relationship is headed in the wrong direction.*

That's where extraordinary effort comes into play. You need to stay focused on your original goal. You need to connect to the vision you had for it, that big *why* in your heart and mind when you set the goal in the first place.

Like me, you need to reverse engineer the goal. Ask yourself, *If I'm at the end of this month and this goal was to have happened, what would I have done? What would I have needed to do?*

Whatever the answer, you will need to stay consistent and persevere, regardless of your results. You have to believe you can still ring the bell of success at the end. You have to maintain unwavering faith and extraordinary effort—until the buzzer sounds. That's the only way that you create an opportunity for the miracle to happen.

Our extraordinary effort is to model the behavior we want from our partner and to create an environment that will enable our relationship to grow. We encourage and support and motivate our partner. We do not use force. Force always backfires. We provide the structure and let our mate have free choice within it.

If you do what the average person does—what our built-in human nature tells us to do—you'll be just like every other average spouse. Don't choose to be that average person! Remember: your thoughts and actions create your results and are therefore a self-fulfilling prophecy. Manage them wisely.

Allow me to introduce you to your edge—the strategy that will practically ensure every one of your goals is realized.

The Miracle Equation

Unwavering Faith + Extraordinary Effort = Miracles

It's easier than you think. The secret to maintaining unwavering faith is to recognize that it's a mindset and a *strategy*—it's not concrete. In fact, it's elusive. You can never make *every* sale. No athlete makes *every* shot. You can never win every battle with your partner. You must program yourself automatically to have the unwavering faith to drive you to keep putting forth the extraordinary effort—regardless of the results.

Remember, the key to putting this equation into practice, to maintaining unwavering faith in the midst of self-doubt, is the Miracle Mantra:

I will _____, no matter what. There is no other option.

Once you set a goal, put that goal into the Miracle Mantra format. Yes, you're going to say your affirmations every morning (and maybe every evening, too). But all day, every day, you're going to repeat your Miracle Mantra to yourself. As you're driving the kids to school or taking the train to the office, while you're on the treadmill, in the shower, in line at the grocery store—in other words: *everywhere you go.*

Your Miracle Mantra will fortify your faith and be the self-talk you need to make just one more try, day after day.

Bonus Lesson

Remember what I learned from my mentor Dan Casetta on the purpose of goals? You have to become the type of person who *can* achieve the goal. You won't always reach the goal, but you can become someone who maintains unwavering faith and puts forth extraordinary effort, regardless of your results. That's how you become the type of person you need to become to achieve extraordinary goals consistently.

And while reaching the goal almost doesn't matter (almost!), more often than not, you'll reach your goal. Do the elite athletes win every time? No. But they win most of the time. And you'll win most of the time, too.

At the end of the day, you can wake up earlier; do the Life S.A.V.E.R.S. with passion and excitement; get organized, focused, and intentional; and master every relationship challenge like a champ. And yet, if you don't combine unwavering faith with extraordinary effort, you won't reach the levels of success you seek.

The Miracle Equation gives you access to forces outside of anyone's understanding, using energy that you might call God, the Universe, the Law of Attraction, or even good luck. I don't know how it works; I just know that it works.

You've read this far—you clearly want success more than almost anything. Commit to following through with every aspect of your relationship, including The Miracle Equation. You deserve it, and I want you to have it!

Putting it into Action:

1. Write out the Miracle Equation and put it where you will see it every day: **Unwavering Faith + Extraordinary Effort = Miracles (UF + EE = M∞)**

2. Determine your number one goal for your relationship this year. What goal, if you were to accomplish it, would bring you closest to your ideal family life?

3. Write your Miracle Mantra: *I will _____ (insert your goals and daily actions here), no matter what. There is no other option.*

It is more about who you become in the process. You'll expand your self-confidence, and, regardless of your results, the very next time you attempt to reach a goal and every time after that, you'll be the type of person who gives it all they've got.

Closing Remarks

Congratulations! You have done what only a small percentage

of people do: read an entire book. If you've come this far, that tells me something about you: you have a thirst for more. You want to become more, do more, contribute more, and earn more.

Right now, you have the unprecedented opportunity to infuse the Life S.A.V.E.R.S. into your life and relationship, upgrade your daily routine, and ultimately upgrade your *life* to a first-class experience beyond your wildest dreams. Before you know it, you will be reaping the astronomical benefits of the habits that top achievers use daily.

Five years from now, your family life, business, relationships, and income will be a direct result of one thing: *who you've become*. It's up to you to wake up each day and dedicate time to becoming the best version of yourself. Seize this moment in time, define a vision for your future, and use what you've learned in this book to turn your vision into your reality.

Imagine a time just a few years from now when you come across the journal you started after completing this book. In it, you find the goals you wrote down for yourself—dreams you didn't dare speak out loud at the time. And as you look around, you realize *your dreams now represent the life you are living*.

Right now, you stand at the foot of a mountain you can easily and effortlessly climb. All you need to do is continue waking up each day for your Miracle Morning and use the Life S.A.V.E.R.S. day after day, month after month, year after year, as you continue to take *yourself*, your *family*, and your *success* to levels beyond what you've ever experienced before.

Combine your Miracle Morning with a commitment to master your Four Relationship Elements and use The Miracle Equation to create results that most people only dream of.

This book was written as an expression of what we know will

work for you, to take every area of your life to the next level faster than you may currently believe is possible. Miraculous performers weren't born that way—they have simply dedicated their lives to developing themselves and their skills to achieve everything they've ever wanted.

You can become one of them, I promise.

Taking Action: The 30-Day Miracle Morning Challenge

Now it is time to join the tens of thousands of people who have transformed their lives with The Miracle Morning. Join the community online at TMMBook.com and download the toolkit to get you started *today*.

ABOUT THE AUTHORS

HAL ELROD is on a mission to *elevate the consciousness of humanity, one morning, one person at a time.* As creator of one of the fastest growing and most engaged online communities in existence and author of one of the highest rated, best-selling books in the world, *The Miracle Morning*—which has been translated into 34 languages, has over 2,000 five-star Amazon reviews and is practiced daily by over 500,000 people in 70+ countries—he is doing exactly that.

What's remarkable is that Hal actually died at age 20. His car was hit head-on by a drunk driver at 70 miles per hour, his heart stopped beating for six minutes, he broke 11 bones and woke up after being in a coma for six days to be told by his doctors that he would never walk again.

Then, in November of 2016, Hal nearly died again—his kidneys, lungs, and heart were all on the verge of failing, and he was diagnosed with a rare, and very aggressive form of cancer and given a 20-30% chance of surviving. After enduring the most difficult year of his life, Hal is now in remission and grateful to be living his mission alongside his wife and their two children in Austin, Texas.

For more information on Hal's keynote speaking, live events, books, and the soon-to-be-released documentary, *The Miracle Morning* (movie), visit HalElrod.com.

LANCE AND BRANDY SALAZAR. Lance was born in California and graduated with a Bachelor's in Chemistry from Fresno State University and a Doctorate in Pharmacy from the University of the Pacific. Brandy was born in California and graduated from, well, Louis Pasteur Jr High School and the School of Hard Knocks. She doesn't have a high school diploma or a college degree. But none of that mattered. They've been married since 2005 and have two beautiful daughters, Hooley and Natalie. Lance spent 20 years as a clinical pharmacist, and Brandy spent 20 very successful years in the real estate investment world. Although they were both very financially and socially prosperous, they were disconnected from each other, not giving their best energy to their marriage. On the brink of divorce, they took a final chance on each other. Taking a different path of designing their marriage the way they wanted it, and through a lot of self-work, they fell back in love.

After resurrecting their relationship, they reconstructed their core values, priorities, and family mission. This led them to quit their careers, sell their "dream" house, get rid of nearly everything they owned, buy a small farmhouse, and begin homeschooling their daughters together.

They created a project called Legendary Couples with Kids to share what they had learned. Their mission is to provide tools and resources to reconnect couples and to keep them connected to each other, where thriving relationships serve as positive examples to their kids and for generations to come. You can learn more at www.legendarycouples.com.

HONORÉE CORDER is the author of dozens of books, including *You Must Write a Book*, *The Prosperous Writers* book series, *Vision to Reality*, *Business Dating*, *The Successful Single Mom* book series, *If Divorce is a Game, These are the Rules*, and *The Divorced Phoenix*. She is also Hal Elrod's business partner in *The Miracle Morning* book series. Honorée coaches business professionals, writers, and aspiring non-fiction authors who want to publish their books to bestseller status, create a platform, and develop multiple streams of income. She also does all sorts of other magical things, and her badassery is legendary. You can find out more at HonoreeCorder.com.

THE MIRACLE MORNING SERIES

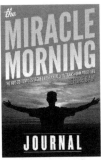

The Journal

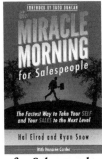

for Salespeople

for Real Estate Agents

for Network Marketers

for Writers

for Entrepreneurs

for Parents & Families

for College Students

THE MIRACLE MORNING SERIES

Millionaires

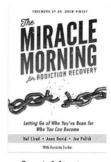

for Addiction Recovery

COMPANION GUIDES & WORKBOOKS

Art of Affirmations

Companion Planner

for Salespeople Companion Guide

for Network Marketers 90-Day Action Plan

for College Student Companion Planner

BOOK HAL to SPEAK

"Bringing Hal in to be the keynote speaker at our annual conference was the best investment we could have made." —**Fidelity National Title**

"Hal was the featured keynote speaker for 400 of our TOP sales performers and executive team. He gave us a plan that was so simple, we had no choice but to put it in action immediately." —**Art Van Furniture**

"Hal received 9.8 out of 10 from our members. That never happens." —**Entrepreneur Organization (NYC Chapter)**

Book Hal as your keynote speaker and you're guaranteed to make your event highly enjoyable and unforgettable!

For more than a decade, **Hal Elrod** has been consistently rated as **the #1 keynote speaker by** meeting planners and attendees.

His unique style combines inspiring audiences with his unbelievable TRUE story, keeping them laughing hysterically with his high-energy, stand-up-comedy-style delivery, and empowering them with actionable strategies to take their *RESULTS* to the *NEXT LEVEL*.

For more info visit **www.HalElrod.com**

HAL ELROD & JON BERGHOFF

PRESENT...

ONE WEEKEND CAN CHANGE YOUR LIFE. JOIN US FOR THIS ONCE-IN-A-LIFETIME EXPERIENCE.

www.BestYearEverLive.com

Most personal development events cause "information overload" and often leave attendees feeling more overwhelmed than when they arrived. You end up with pages and pages of notes, then you go home and have to figure out how and when to implement everything you've learned.

Co-hosted by experiential trainer, Jon Berghoff, the **Best Year Ever Blueprint LIVE** event won't just teach you how to change your life, you'll actually starting taking steps to *change your life while you're still at the event*.

"I truly had a life changing weekend during BYEB2015. I feel as if my mind has hit a 'reset' button. Reading The Miracle Morning and coming to the live event has been a gift, and the best investment in myself I've ever made. I am excited to take this momentum and create my level 10 life next year!"

–Ericka Staples

Learn more about
the Best Year Everevent online at
WWW.BESTYEAREVERLIVE.COM

Printed in Great Britain
by Amazon